fear-free food

fear-free food

How to ditch dieting
and fall back in love with food

NICOLA JANE HOBBS

GREEN TREE
LONDON · OXFORD · NEW YORK · NEW DELHI · SYDNEY

For those who want to live with
less fear and more freedom

GREEN TREE
Bloomsbury Publishing Plc
50 Bedford Square, London, WC1B 3DP, UK

BLOOMSBURY, GREEN TREE and the Diana logo are trademarks of Bloomsbury Publishing Plc

First published in Great Britain in 2018

A catalogue record for this book is available from the British Library
Library of Congress Cataloguing-in-Publication data has been applied for
ISBN: PB: 9781472950178; eBook: 9781472950185

2 4 6 8 10 9 7 5 3 1

Designed by Matt Windsor
Printed and bound in the UK by Bell & Bain Ltd
Food styling by Emily Kydd
All food photography and author portrait on page 15 by Clare Winfield
Author portraits on pages 31, 39, 45, 49, 64 and 200 by Glen Burrows
Illustrations compiled by D.R.ink/iStock
Images on pages 54 and 70 © Getty Images

To find out more about our authors and books visit www.bloomsbury.com and sign up for our newsletters.

Contents

ABOUT THE AUTHOR

Nicola's passion is helping people eat, move and live with less fear and more freedom. She has a Master's degree in psychology, specialising in Eating and Exercise Psychology and is a qualified nutritionist and certified Intuitive Eating Counselor. Nicola also teaches yoga internationally and is the author of *Thrive Through Yoga* and *Yoga Gym*, both published by Bloomsbury. www.NicolaJaneHobbs.com.

INTRODUCTION

Fear-Free Philosophy

When I was consumed by my own struggles with food, I vowed that if I ever found freedom, I would write a book to help others find freedom too. *Fear-Free Food* is that book. It can be summarised by the following statement:

> ## Eat freely. Love fiercely. Live fearlessly.

This is the philosophy of the whole book in a nutshell. Forget fad diets, clean eating and banning entire food groups, these six words are the short answer to the seemingly endless and confusing questions of what, why and how we should eat in order to be as healthy and happy as we can.

Eating freely refers to eating in a nourishing and self-loving way, having freedom from self-imposed food rules and restrictions, letting go of guilt and fear around eating, and celebrating food as a way to add meaning to your life.

Loving fiercely is about loving and respecting your body enough to make food choices that nourish you and leave you feeling healthy and energised.

And *living fearlessly* signifies how healing your relationship with food will empower you to become stronger and braver in other areas of your life.

Dieting, meal skipping and food restricting are so entrenched in our culture that they have become normal. We 'eat clean', avoid carbs and eliminate 'forbidden' foods. We cut out sugar and gluten and dairy. We jump from one fad diet or lifestyle trend to the next in search of the 'perfect' diet in the hope that it will give us the perfect body, perfect health and, ultimately, a perfect life. And millions of us are slaves to this diet culture where eating stresses us out and feeling guilt, confusion and anxiety around food is an everyday occurrence.

I spent years on the dieting, clean-eating, calorie-counting bandwagon and it didn't make me any healthier or happier. So I've written *Fear-Free Food* to show you that there is another way. I want to show you that you can stop dieting, trust your body and still reach your health and fitness goals. My aim is to show you how to make peace with food, honour your hunger and eat in a way that feels natural to you.

Fear-Free Food is part of a new anti-diet paradigm – a revolutionary non-diet eating movement that will empower you to remove all the rules and restrictions around food, respect your body and become healthier and happier. It's about replacing dieting and deprivation with nutrition and nourishment. It's about reigniting your passion, enjoyment and excitement for cooking and eating with heaps of delicious recipes. Ultimately, it's about eating with less fear and more freedom.

Aim

I created *Fear-Free Food* because I was tired of reading conflicting nutrition information. I was fed up with being told that I should 'stand away from the buffet table' at parties, that enjoying a slice of cake over coffee with a friend would make me fat and that celebrating food is at odds with health. I was tired of hearing that social gatherings involving food were problematic, that I should replace my favourite chocolate brownies with gluten-free, sugar-free, dairy-free ones, and that healthy eating requires willpower, self-denial and self-control. It upset me to discover the number of people who feel guilt and anxiety around food and it forced me to question why, despite all the scientific advances, nutrition research and expert advice, we are still deliberating over which foods are good for us and which ones aren't. And while we're deliberating, rates of obesity, eating disorders and diet-related diseases are higher than ever before.

Unless our approach to eating and exercise changes, over 40 per cent of the UK population and 50 per cent of people in the USA are predicted to be obese by 2030. And with this, millions more cases of lifestyle-related diseases including diabetes, heart disease, cancer, high blood pressure and osteoarthritis are expected too. The same is true for eating disorders with an estimated 6 per cent of adults suffering from eating disorders in the UK and USA – that's over 22 million people. These statistics highlight how our current culture of dieting and deprivation is just not working. It's time for a less restrictive and more compassionate approach to eating.

From my own journey and those of my clients, I've learned that we don't have to choose between being healthy and eating freely. We don't have to count every calorie, ban entire food groups and meticulously measure portion sizes in order to

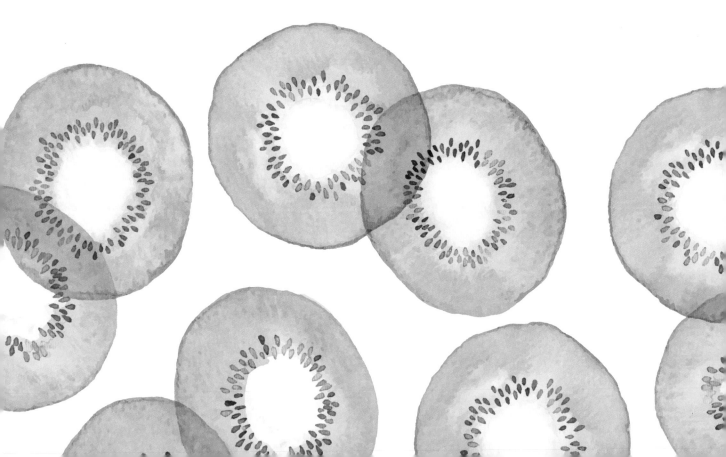

look and feel our best. Despite what the media, diet industry and many healthy eating books and wellness blogs have led us to believe, we can be healthy, happy, eat freely and enjoy our food without obsession, restriction, anxiety or guilt.

Fear-Free Food is an alternative to dieting and clean eating. It is a new and liberating way of relating to food that focuses on improving health and happiness without the need to restrict food groups, control portion sizes or obsess over calories. It is a non-diet approach that will help you make peace with food, rediscover the joys of eating, and become more self-aware and self-accepting – not just with food but with your body, yourself and your life as a whole.

It has the following aims:

1. To give you the practical steps to build a fear-free relationship with food.
2. To simplify nutrition and dispel widespread nutrition myths so you can choose foods that you know will nourish you.
3. To inspire you with oodles of delicious recipes.

There is an aura of elitism around eating well and many experts promote their method as the best way to lose weight/get healthy/feel great. They often provide generic meal plans and one-size-fits-all principles backed up by cherry-picked data. I wanted to make sure that *Fear-Free Food* was not like that. It is not a cookie-cutter approach (although I do like cookies!). There is no judgement if you do or do not choose to eat meat or dairy or sugar. And there are no rules to follow or meal plans to stick to.

Instead, *Fear-Free Food* is an insight, an understanding, a new way of eating, of relating to food and seeing yourself and the world. I'm not going to tell you what you should or shouldn't eat; instead, I'm going to provide you with knowledge, tools and guidance so you can make your own food choices and begin to eat in the way that works for you. I'm also going to give you the practical steps to

break free from the diet mentality, and I have included over 80 nutritious and delicious recipes, so you can put this knowledge into action. I want to empower you to experience the joy, connection and excitement that food can bring to your life, so, ultimately you can become healthier and happier.

While introducing what *Fear-Free Food* is, I would also like to highlight what *Fear-Free Food* is not. One backlash to the clean-eating trend is a growing phenomenon which replaces wellness with indulgence: kale smoothies with extravagant milkshakes, and quinoa with bacon-laden burgers. Now, I love having a burger from time to time (and there are some delicious burger recipes on pages 142, 156, 160, 170), but the idea that we need to rebel against dieting and clean eating by promoting gluttony is just as extreme and will not help you become healthier or happier. So, *Fear-Free Food* is not:

✪ An excuse for overindulgence;
✪ A total disregard for nutrition and how amazing nourishing food can make you feel;
✪ A list of rules and instructions on what you should and shouldn't eat;
✪ A quick fix;
✪ A weight-loss plan.

I've shared a lot of my own personal experiences and those of my clients throughout the book because I've found that we can learn a lot from other people's stories. While I am a researcher and a professional in nutrition and psychology, I'm not writing this book as an objective scientist or detached researcher. I'm writing it as an eater – just like you. And I hope that by me sharing my story, you will gain a greater understanding of yourself, your relationship with food and how you can eat freely, love fiercely and live fearlessly.

My Story

I wanted to share my story so you know that you are not alone. Our relationship with food, weight and our body is so personal to each of us that we often end up hiding our struggles and insecurities out of fear of being judged as greedy, undisciplined, vain or out of control. So, we keep our body insecurities, obsessive dieting and unhealthy food habits a secret. And, because we keep them a secret, we live with fear, guilt and shame; afraid of food, feeling guilty about what we eat and ashamed about the number on the scales and the reflection we see in the mirror.

I've had a pretty turbulent relationship with food in the past. From the age of 14 until my early twenties, I struggled intensely with food. You name the eating issue, I've dealt with it: meal skipping, obsessive calorie counting, elimination diets, clean eating, anorexia, orthorexia, over-exercise, emotional eating, weight gain, weight loss… So I want to reassure you that I understand. I get it. I've felt the anxiety and the guilt and the shame. I've experienced the nutritional confusion, body-shaming thoughts and all-consuming cravings.

Trust me, you are not alone in this.

HOW IT ALL STARTED

Up until I was 14 I had never counted a calorie in my life. I ate when I was hungry and stopped when I was full. I never had any digestive issues or intolerances. I effortlessly maintained a healthy weight, enjoyed a variety of sports and never really thought that much about what I ate other than whether or not it tasted good.

Dieting was something I fell into by mistake. I don't know the reasons why, and I'm not sure it matters all that much now, but I started restricting my food – first by cutting out chocolate and crisps, then skipping lunch at school and then purposefully limiting calories and exercising more. My weight dropped and by the time I was 15 I had been diagnosed with anorexia. I spent the next four years trapped in a cycle of hospital refeeding regimes only to come out of each hospital admission still consumed by anxiety around food. None of the things that were supposed to help (therapy, drugs, psychoanalysis, dealing with emotional issues, boosting my self-esteem…) ever worked. At 19, my weight had dropped so low I suffered organ failure. It was a big wake-up call and I managed to get my weight up to a level that, while not healthy, at least allowed me to function day-to-day. Although I was no longer at physical risk, for the next couple of years my relationship with food was far from healthy. I became trapped in a world of clean eating, calorie counting and sugar-free, gluten-free, dairy-free dieting because I thought it would make me healthier and happier. In fact, it just made me neurotic, obsessive and overly anxious about food.

CHRONIC DIETING AND CLEAN EATING

Dieting and the pursuit of thinness are entrenched in the Western diet culture and I got sucked in big time. I thought that my diet was a reflection of my worth and that the 'cleaner' I ate and the more I cut out sugar, gluten, meat and anything processed, the better I was as a person. I thought that as long as I controlled my calorie intake and placed food in strict categories of 'good' and 'bad', the less overwhelming and more manageable life would be.

I attempted numerous fad diets inspired by books, blogs and social media. There was the time when I cut out all carbs because I'd read in a magazine that they make you store fat around your belly. Then there was the time when I made sure I had six meals a day because someone had told me my metabolism would slow down if I didn't. There was also the time when I cut out all gluten and grains because I saw an article online that said they destroyed your gut. And then there was the time when I weighed and tracked every single thing I ate because I thought my appetite couldn't be trusted.

When I wasn't worrying about what I ate for breakfast, I was worrying about what I was going to have for lunch, or if I had gone over my allotted calories for the day, or if my oats had gluten in them. But, underneath it all, my real worry was that I'd be imprisoned by these unhealthy eating habits forever.

Eating clean, counting calories and creating more and more rules around food might have made me feel in control, but what I really wanted was freedom. Freedom from anxiety. Freedom from guilt. Freedom from obsession. Freedom from the thoughts that told me that carbs were the devil, eating sugar would make me fat and that I needed to keep a tight harness on my appetite at all times. Deep down, I wanted the freedom to trust my body, truly nourish myself and enjoy my life to the fullest.

And that freedom does exist. Because I have found it.

HOW I FOUND FREEDOM

After going through anorexia and being told by doctors and therapists that I'd have food issues my whole life and they were 'just something I'd have to manage', I accepted that I would spend the rest of my life fearing food and battling my body. But, I can tell you now that nothing could be further from the truth.

It was the following two insights that set me free from my food fears and allowed me to rebuild a healthy relationship with eating, my body and myself:

1. The dieting industry is wrong

We've been led to believe that we need to live by a set of food rules because, if we don't, we'll lose control, eat everything in sight and gain a tonne of weight. We've been sucked into thinking that our bodies can't be trusted and instead we need to rely on scientific research, dietary guidelines, food labelling and perplexing pyramids. One minute scientists are telling us to cut out fat and the next we're being told to put coconut oil in our coffee. The dieting industry has convinced us that as long as we follow a set of food rules, cut out specific food groups and maybe add in a 'superfood' or two, then we'll be healthier and happier.

Well, I spent nearly a decade listening to the diet industry. And do you know what I learned? Many of the so-called 'experts' are wrong. I found that the more I cut out food groups, counted calories and went hungry because the latest diet said you should fast for 16 hours, or swap carbs for cauliflower, or cut out sugar because it's 'toxic', the lousier my life became. Restricting my food restricted my life.

2. I am the expert of my body

There are a lot of experts out there who know a lot about food. But I realised that *I* am the expert of my body. Just as *you* are the expert of your body.

This insight transformed my relationship with food in an instant. Only *I* knew which foods made me feel energised and which ones made me feel sluggish. Only *I* could tell when I was hungry and when I was full. Only *I* could recognise whether I was eating for physical or emotional reasons. Only *I* was aware of whether counting calories and cutting out food groups was helpful or harmful. And only *I* could decide to make peace with food, honour my appetite and nourish myself properly.

So, I put a giant middle finger up to dieting, gave myself unconditional permission to eat and began learning how to trust my body. I have never looked back.

Of course, after years of restricting, obsessing and relating my diet to my self-worth, it took time and practice to rebuild a healthy relationship with food. But I made the decision to let go of all the food rules and restrictions I'd developed over the years and instead simplified my diet in the direction of fresh, natural and delicious foods – the very foods my body was intuitively drawn towards. And, as I did this, I found I became more sensitive to my body's needs and I learned that I didn't need experts to tell me what to eat after all.

As well as letting go of the rules I had created around my diet, I explored mind-body practices like yoga and meditation to free me from my anxiety around food, weight and my body. And I also began applying the neuroscientific information I researched during my master's degree on the psychology of eating and exercise to help me escape the diet mentality I'd been sucked into. I learned that a lot of the confusion, anxiety and guilt I had around food were things I could unlearn. These thoughts and feelings were simply destructive messages I'd absorbed from our diet culture that had become so automatic I had forgotten what it was like to eat what I actually enjoyed instead of eating what I thought I 'should' eat. I began to separate my real yearning to be happy and healthy from the paranoid and untrue thoughts that said: 'You'll get fat if you eat carbs', 'You have no willpower if you eat more than 1200 calories a day' and 'Eating processed foods means you're lazy.'

I began to see that I didn't have to spend the rest of my life counting calories, fearing fat or keeping a tight rein on my appetite. Rather than acting on thoughts that told me I needed to 'be thinner' or 'eat cleaner' by jumping on the next dieting bandwagon,

I was able to dismiss these anxieties and continue to nourish myself properly.

By using various spiritual and scientific strategies, I stopped letting food, and my anxieties around it, have power over me. I began eating with less fear and more freedom.

I explore some of these spiritual and scientific strategies in Part 1 – Fear-Free Eating (pages 21–53). And, if you are interested in learning more about the neuroscience of eating and how to use the power of your brain to escape the cycle of dieting, you can find more information and techniques at: www.FearFreeFood.co.uk.

WHERE I AM NOW

Rebuilding a healthy relationship with food was pretty simple when I knew how. For years, I had known deep down that restricting food, fighting my appetite and jumping from one fad diet to the next was not bringing me the health or happiness I truly wanted, but I didn't know there was another way. Although it felt harsh and restrictive, I didn't see there was a better option. But now I know there is – an approach that allows me to trust my appetite and eat without rules and restrictions.

I have learned to relate to food in a new, healthier, more balanced way that doesn't involve anxiety, obsession or guilt. I have realised that I can eat in a way that feels natural to me without losing control, becoming addicted to sugar, getting bloated, breaking out in spots, damaging my gut or gaining a tonne of weight (like the media and diet industry often lead us to believe).

I am no longer a slave to a diet culture that encourages self-deprivation and restriction for the sake of health. And my relationship with food is fear-free.

I don't have the 'perfect' diet and nor do I want one. Instead I eat whatever the heck I want, I feel strong and healthy, and I maintain my weight effortlessly through fear-free eating and regular exercise.

As a side note, eating 'whatever the heck I want' doesn't mean I live off takeaway pizza and binge on biscuits. It means I eat food that makes me feel happy, energised and full of life. Usually this means fresh, natural, nutrient-rich food, but sometimes I choose to eat too much chocolate, and I don't think twice about enjoying an ice cream on the beach in the summer or ordering a slice of freshly baked cake with my coffee. Whether it's a hearty bowl of lentil soup, a juicy fruit salad or a gooey chocolate brownie, whatever food choice I make, I embrace it without fear or guilt.

I refuse to allow anxiety, rules or guilt to guide my food choices anymore so, instead, I am guided by how I want to feel – strong, powerful and free. I use food to nourish myself instead of being an outlet for self-control. And I am enjoying exploring what food makes me feel my best. Here is what I've discovered works for me so far...

I feel good:
✪ starting my day with a mug of herbal tea;
✪ having three nourishing meals a day;
✪ eating dinner before 8 p.m.;
✪ basing my meals around plants and beans;
✪ eating cooked vegetables instead of raw salads;
✪ cooking with spices like chilli and turmeric.

I don't feel good:
✪ having caffeine past 3 p.m. as it stops me sleeping;
✪ eating cow's cheese (so I choose goat's cheese);
✪ grazing on lots of small meals and snacks throughout the day;
✪ eating lots of meat because it makes me feel sluggish;
✪ drinking alcohol when I'm home alone;
✪ eating when I'm standing up, in a rush or stressed.

This is just what works for *me* (and I'm still learning!). These are certainly not rules and I'm not saying that these things will work for you. But I wanted to share what I've learned so you can get a feel for how, like me, your relationship with food can transform from one of control, restriction and paranoia, to one that is driven by self-love, nourishment and freedom.

This is what *Fear-Free Food* is all about – letting go of rules and restrictions, exploring new foods, becoming curious about what makes your body feel good, and eating without fear or guilt so you can fall back in love with food, your body and your life.

Throughout my journey I've learned that eating a healthy diet and being a healthy weight doesn't have to be such a struggle. It doesn't have to be about control and self-denial or revolve around meal plans and restrictive diets. The philosophies, tools and recipes you'll find in this book are those I've learned through my own journey, my training in nutrition, degrees in psychology, work with clients, speaking with professionals, and from published research on nutrition, body image and eating psychology.

On the following pages, you'll find scientific information about nutrition so you can make informed choices about what to eat. I have also outlined simple steps that will teach you how to eat without guilt, fear and anxiety, and there are over 80 delicious and nutritious recipes so you can easily implement *Fear-Free Food* every day.

This is not just about eating fear-free food, this is about living a fear-free life.

Who This Book is For

This book is for anyone who is tired of fad diets and clean eating. It's for anyone who wants to feel healthier and happier without food rules and dietary restrictions. Whether you want to ease your anxiety around food, feel healthier, get stronger, stop binging or simply explore nutritious and delicious recipes, *Fear-Free Food* gives you a fun, creative and nourishing way to transform your relationship with food, your body and your life.

Fear-Free Food is a gentler, kinder alternative to dieting that doesn't come with the usual side effects: poor body image, low self-esteem, anxiety, depression, unhealthy eating behaviours, long-term weight gain, and disordered eating symptoms to name just a few.

Being on a diet is now promoted as so normal that some of my clients don't even realise they've been sucked into one! Rules and restrictions, anxiety and guilt, and preoccupation with dieting and weight control can feel so normal that it's easy to forget what it's like to live without a dieting mentality.

Self-awareness is the first step to freedom. See if you can relate to any of the following statements to become aware of how dieting beliefs and unhealthy eating habits could be limiting your health and happiness:

- ✪ I have dieted on and off for years and follow rules on what I can and can't eat.
- ✪ I don't trust my appetite and beat myself up if I eat more than I had planned to or break the rules of my diet.
- ✪ I feel lack of willpower stops me from reaching my health, fitness and weight goals.
- ✪ I avoid certain food groups such as carbs, processed foods and foods containing gluten, sugar or dairy.
- ✪ I spend a lot of time researching the nutritional value of foods and see foods as healthy or unhealthy.
- ✪ I have a lot of negative feelings around eating, like guilt, shame, and remorse, and can feel out of control when I eat.

So, if you can relate to any of the above statements and you would like to break free from the trap of dieting so you can eat in a way that feels natural, this book is for *you*.

How This Book Works

This book is divided into three main sections. The first two sections give you the tools to build a healthy relationship with food and the knowledge to eat in a way that nourishes you. The last section gives you heaps of delicious and nutritious recipes. You don't have to read the book in order, so, if you're keen to get cooking right away then feel free to skip straight to *Fear-Free Recipes* (see pages 71–199) and read over the first parts of the book whenever you have time.

Part 1: *Fear-Free Eating* will introduce you to why we eat and why we worry about what we eat. It will look at traditional diets from the healthiest and happiest nations in the world as well as why so many of us feel guilty about what we eat. It will explore diet culture in the 21st century and how and why so many of us have been led to believe we need to eat clean, go vegan, cut out gluten, or follow whatever the latest diet trend is in order to be healthy. It'll compare *fear-based eating* to *fear-free eating* and give you the practical tools to free yourself from the diet mentality and rebuild a healthy relationship with food.

Part 2: *Fear-Free Nutrition* will break down widespread myths around food. It will simplify nutrition by providing information on calories, nutrients, superfoods, and common fear foods such as gluten, dairy, sugar, and processed foods.

Part 3: *Fear-Free Recipes* takes up the bulk of the book because the best way to rebuild a healthy relationship with food is to start experimenting and having fun with it. It gives you over 80 delicious recipes designed so you can eat with less fear and more freedom. There is an introduction to cooking and each of the recipes has been created with five things in mind: pleasure, nutrition, practicality, connection, and tradition. The aim of *Fear-Free Recipes* is to give you inspiration and confidence in cooking so food is no longer a source of anxiety or obsession, but instead becomes a way to find trust in your body, nourish yourself, express your creativity, connect with others, and find balance in your life.

FEAR-FREE FOOD...

...is for anyone who has ever struggled with food, weight and body image, is fed up with strict diets and restrictive regimes, and wants to eat with less anxiety and guilt and more enjoyment and freedom.

...is for anyone who wants to escape the cycle of fad diets and rule-based eating, learn to trust their body, and become healthier and happier while doing so.

...is part of the anti-diet paradigm that focuses on replacing dieting and deprivation with nutrition and nourishment.

...gives you the practical steps to build a fear-free relationship with food, simplifies nutrition so you can choose foods that you know will nourish you, and provides you with heaps of delicious recipes.

*...is divided into three main sections: **Fear-Free Eating, Fear-Free Nutrition**, and **Fear-Free Recipes**.*

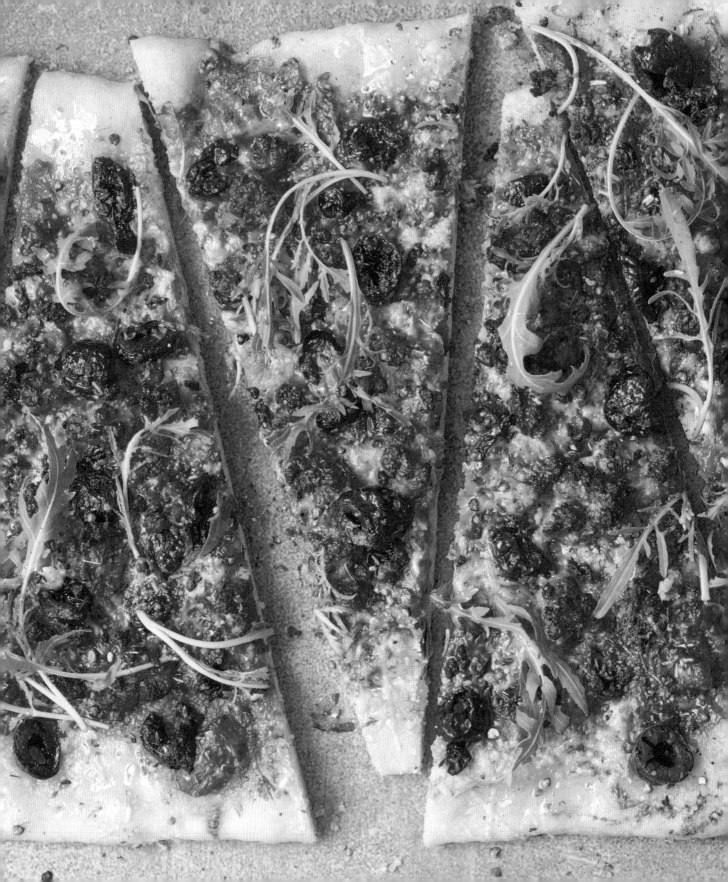

PART 1
FEAR-FREE EATING

Understanding why we eat, what we eat and why we worry about what we eat, can help us to understand the role food plays in our lives. This can be extremely helpful when it comes to rebuilding a fear-free relationship with food. Rather than getting more and more bogged down by conflicting nutrition messages and the latest miracle diets, it is helpful to take a step back and look briefly at food from a historical and cultural perspective. By understanding this, we can then build a relationship with food that, rather than being driven by the scaremongering of the diet industry, is instead guided by trust in our body and confidence in the amazing ability of food to make us healthier and happier.

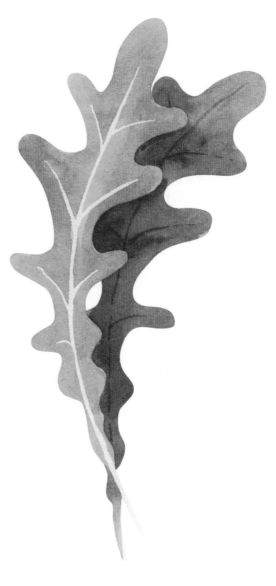

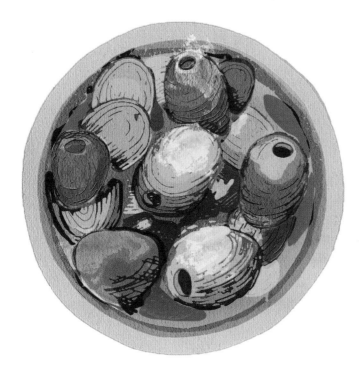

What We Eat

Looking through a handful of bestselling healthy-eating cookbooks highlights why we need to change the way we see food if we want to have a healthy relationship with it. One book recommends cutting out sugar because it's a drug that will make you fat, avoiding gluten because it can destroy your gut and giving up dairy because it can make you bloated. Another book says gluten and sugar are okay but we need to limit meat, cheese and all animal products. And another one states that eating animal protein will help us feel fuller for longer, so we need to eat more of it if we want to escape the cycle of yo-yo dieting. Confused? I certainly am!

Up until fairly recently, we relied on culture and tradition to guide our food choices. Now, we're looking to scientists, experts, and even bloggers for guidance instead. We eat 'scientifically' and/or 'fashionably'. Whether we realise it or not, we are influenced by the latest food fads, which have been shaped by the food industry and media. I'm sure we all know someone who has cut out carbs because they read on a blog they make you gain weight, has gone sugar-free because they read in a magazine it was 'toxic' or swapped spaghetti for 'courgetti' (spiralised courgette) because that's what their favourite social media influencer is sharing on Instagram.

No other animal needs scientific advice to tell it what to eat and, in reality, nutrition science is still too young to tell us much definitively. Of course we can learn a lot from science, but we can learn just as much, if not more, from tradition.

TRADITIONAL DIETS
People across the globe follow a huge variety of diets largely because of their environment and traditions. For example, traditional food in India includes lentils, spices and ghee; in England it includes meat and potatoes; and in the Middle East it's falafel, hummus and legumes. These native foods are part of the traditional diets that nourished our ancestors before the industrialisation of food and have been passed down through generations. Traditional diets like these were based on what people could grow, forage or hunt from their natural environment and, without any thought to calories or superfoods, these people still went on to live healthy lives.

Dan Buettner, a renowned explorer and researcher for *National Geographic*, looked at the role of traditional diets in health and longevity in his research on the Blue Zones – the five places in the world where people live the longest and, according to his research, are the happiest and healthiest. The five areas he identified are: the Barbagia region of Sardinia, the Greek island of Ikaria, the Nicoya Peninsula in Costa Rica, Loma Linda in California, and Okinawa – an island off Japan. Buettner and his team of researchers found that, although the diets of these populations vary considerably because of the environments in each country (for example, Okinawans eat a diet high in tofu, sweet potatoes and turmeric, while the Ikarian diet revolves largely around beans and greens), there were some simple dietary trends across all five Blue Zones that contributed to the populations' longevity:

- Basing your meals around plants and beans.
- Drinking a small amount of wine regularly with friends and family.
- Eating until you are 80 per cent full instead of feeling stuffed.

It is interesting to note that the other six commonalities of the world's longest-lived people were not diet-related at all! Instead, they included:

- moving naturally;
- having a sense of purpose and a feeling of belonging;
- practising stress-reducing routines and habits;
- putting loved ones first;
- having social circles that support healthy behaviours.

Pasta making in Sardinia with 82-year old Auntie Annarita and her family. You can find the recipe for Malloreddus (Sardinian Pasta Shells) on page 175.

for convenience, changing work patterns impinge on family meal times, and life has become busier and we feel forced to multitask (so we eat when we're also working). But it might also be because many of the countless diets we are following and intolerances we seem to have developed make it impossible to share food. I remember a time when I would always organise to see friends and family outside of mealtimes so I didn't have to battle with finding a gluten-free vegan dish on the menu. Now that I have no self-imposed food rules or restrictions, I love nothing more than hosting dinner parties, going out for girly brunches and meeting my mum for tea and cake.

Stumbling across the research on the Blue Zones a few years ago made me realise that worrying unnecessarily about how 'clean' my diet was meant I was neglecting other areas of my life that could make me happier, such as family, stress reduction and finding my purpose. My quest to find the perfect diet wasn't working and was actually having a negative effect on my health. Sometimes the rules and restrictions that surround our food choices can be so consuming that we end up sacrificing the very things that will make us healthier and happier.

THE MODERN WESTERN DIET

In the UK and USA today many of our meals are eaten alone. A recent study looking at British meal patterns found that, in the UK, we now eat around one-third of our meals alone. And similar research carried out in the USA found that over 50 per cent of meals are eaten alone in America. Instead of cooking and sharing a meal as a couple or sitting down for dinner as a family and talking about our day, many of us now grab food and eat in front of the TV, at our desks or on the move. This is partly because more people live alone and choose ready-prepared meals

What is promoted as a 'healthy' diet in the West in comparison to the diets of non-Western cultures is also interesting. When I was at the peak of my pointless quest for nutritional perfection, I became even more confused when some experts were promoting high-protein and high-meat diets, while others were encouraging vegan diets full of starchy carbs. For example, some acclaimed doctors and health experts advocate a protein-rich diet for its health benefits while others blame eating too much protein for the rise in obesity and diet-related diseases. And the myriad perplexing plates and pyramids the government use to illustrate what makes up a healthy diet can be equally puzzling. These plates and pyramids change in accordance with shifts in scientific opinion and have been criticised by health experts for being based on shaky scientific evidence and conveying the wrong dietary advice.

So you can see how easy it is to end up in a state of nutritional confusion!

Why We Eat

Up until a couple of years ago, I never even considered there would be any reason to eat other than for physical health. I saw my body as a machine and I wanted to make sure I was giving it the cleanest, purest fuel possible. What I neglected to understand is that food is much more than just fuel, it is full of meaning and emotion. And, as long as we channel that meaning in nourishing and self-loving directions, we can use food as a way to connect with others and with the world, and become healthier on all levels – physically, mentally, emotionally, spiritually and socially.

I'm not saying that being mindful of our physical health when we make food choices is not important (I go into the importance of being aware of, but not obsessed by, the effect food can have on our health and energy in Part 2 – Fear-Free Nutrition, pages 55–69), but it's good to be reminded that eating for reasons other than physical health will not make us any less healthy.

HEALTH AND NUTRITION

We all have our own beliefs about which foods contribute to our health and which ones aren't so nutritious. Some of these are based on facts, while some of them are based on misinformation that has been manipulated or exaggerated by the media. We might have an arbitrary number of calories we try and stay under, or we avoid foods that have lots of saturated fat in them, or we restrict carbs. Most of these ideas that consciously or subconsciously guide our food choices originate from nutritional science.

As a concept, nutrients (the chemical components of food, including protein, fats, carbs, fibre and vitamins) have been around since the early 19th century. But it wasn't until the 1980s that the food and diet industry began marketing this scientific view of food. Terms that your everyday eater had never heard before – like 'fibre' and 'saturated fat' – started to appear on food packaging with promises of improved health. Eating food was replaced by the idea that we eat

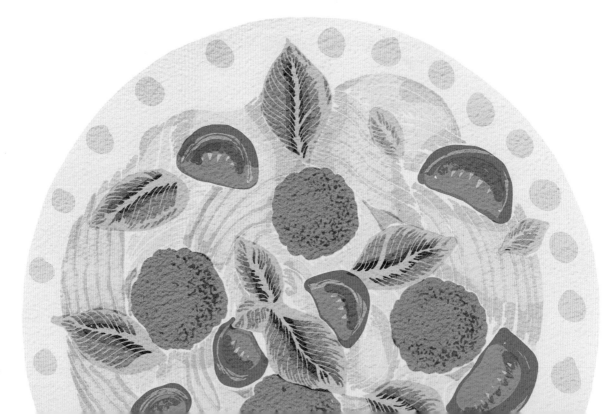

nutrients, and food was quickly categorised as 'good' or 'bad' depending on the nutrients it contained.

The term 'nutritionism' was coined by Gyory Scrinis, an expert in the science and politics of dietary advice, in 2002. It describes the way in which we now make a lot of our food choices based *only* on the nutrients they do or don't contain rather than considering other ways food can nourish us (for example, socially and sensually). I'm sure we've all been sucked in by 'low-fat' or 'high protein' claims printed on the front of food packets at one point or another.

However, what I've learned on my journey to overcoming my anxiety around eating is that we need to appreciate food for more than its nutritional content if we want to have a healthy relationship with it.

Even in the anti-diet paradigm of *Fear-Free Food*, understanding the basics of nutrition can be helpful when making food choices that will make us feel great. But, focusing *solely* on nutrition can foster anxiety around eating because nutrients are a scientific concept that can be difficult to understand – even scientists disagree with each other! Nutrient obsession also encourages food fads; there always seems to be one evil nutrient and one hero nutrient depending on the latest headlines. After years of being demonised, fat seems to have become one of the heroes in recent years. We're seeing fat-rich foods like avocados, nuts and coconut oil being hailed as superfoods by the media, and experts are even suggesting that a high-fat diet could be helpful in curing diabetes.

I find that my clients' relationship with food improves hugely when they stop looking at food solely as a collection of nutrients to control and manipulate. In reality, it's of limited use to look at nutrients outside the context of food, food outside the context of meals, meals outside the context of diets, diets outside the context of lifestyles, and lifestyles outside the context of culture. At the end of the day, we don't eat nutrients – we eat food.

PLEASURE

Another thing that has an impact on food choice is the pleasure and enjoyment we get from it. But with a diet culture that promotes self-sacrifice and self-denial in the name of health, it is easy to feel guilty about loving food and finding joy in eating. And many of us are afraid that if we allow ourselves to really enjoy our food, we'll never be able to stop eating!

In reality, research suggests that when we savour our food and really enjoy the tastes and textures, we're less likely to overeat because we satisfy all our senses. So, if you fancy some ice cream, rather than scoffing it down quickly in front of the freezer because you feel guilty about eating it and worrying about every mouthful, place a couple of scoops in a pretty bowl, add some fruit or drizzle over some sauce to make it look beautiful, and sit down and really enjoy it.

I used to believe that instead of trusting my taste buds and simply eating what I enjoyed, I had to follow nutrition rules if I wanted to be healthy. As a kid, I used to love hot cross buns, but as I became more paranoid about the healthiness of food, I remember numerous times where I turned down a freshly baked hot cross bun, because: a) I was scared about the sugar/gluten/dairy/unknown calories in it; b) I had been swept up into a nutrition mindset where the only purpose of food is to satisfy physiological needs and therefore flavour and pleasure had no place in eating; and c) I thought eating purely for the sake of pleasure meant I was out of control, weak and greedy for 'giving in' to the foods I enjoyed.

However, I've since learned that pleasure brings peace. When I allowed myself to enjoy a toasted hot cross bun with a cup of tea on a relaxing Sunday morning, I found my anxiety around food reduced. When I stopped basing my meals on how 'clean' they were, I learned that enjoying what I was eating didn't mean I would lose control of my appetite and overeat. Nor did it mean I was greedy or immoral. All it meant

Afternoon tea with my family. One of my favourite memories in the whole world.

was that I was replacing my daily dose of mealtime anxiety with positive, enjoyable experiences.

The research on eating psychology backs up my own experiences. A body of research comparing people's attitude to food in France and the USA shows that the French view food as a form of pleasure and celebration whereas Americans link it with guilt and stress. The French also appear to pay more attention to the taste, texture and smell of foods than its nutritional properties and are less concerned about the health consequences of what they eat than Americans, yet they have lower rates of obesity and heart disease. Rather than being caught up in diet trends and clean eating, the French, as a nation, seem to have created a healthier attitude towards food – one which is based on balance and moderation. They don't diet as much as Americans, they don't feel as guilty, they eat slowly, they focus on the social aspects of eating and they pay more attention when they are eating. All this means that the French

get more enjoyment out of less food (more 'food experience') – eating mindfully and savouring their food helps them tune into their body's hunger and fullness signals and stops them overeating.

Research exploring why most dieters are unable to follow their diet long-term found that dieters who restrict food and ignore the pleasurable aspects of eating experience more spontaneous hedonic thoughts about food (random thoughts about the deliciousness of food) than non-dieters – likely triggers for overeating. I know that whenever I restricted my food I used to crave all the things I didn't allow myself: when I was following a low-carb diet, I would crave toasties; when I was only eating raw foods, I would crave a steaming hot bowl of soup; and when I was restricting my calories, I pretty much craved everything! Now that I allow myself to eat freely, I rarely have cravings at all. And if I do, I trust my body and allow myself to eat what I fancy, knowing that I won't overeat.

CONNECTION

Some of my happiest memories in life revolve around food. One is when my dad treated me and my twin sister to afternoon tea at a posh hotel in London for our birthday. The whole family got together and we spent a couple of hours talking, laughing and connecting while drinking tea, sipping on champagne and tucking into sandwiches, scones and the most beautiful cakes I have ever eaten.

These kinds of memories highlight how food is so much more than nutrition; it is a vehicle for communication and connection, a way to express our creativity and maintain traditions, and a tool to create memories. Whether it's getting together with your family over Sunday lunch, going on a date to a nice restaurant with your partner or baking muffins with your kids, food gives us an opportunity to escape our busy, overscheduled lives to not just eat, but to share, connect and nurture our relationships.

If you're worried that shifting the focus of food away from health and towards connection means you'll become less healthy, don't be. A body of research has found that family meals encourage good nutrition, support mental health, and can be protective against obesity and disordered eating, such as chronic dieting, meal skipping and emotional eating.

Using food as a way to connect instead of as an outlet for self-control is one of the simplest and most enjoyable ways we can not only improve our health, but also heal our relationship with food.

NATURE

A few years ago, my daily diet consisted of high-protein shakes, low-calorie cereal bars and 'healthy' ready meals because I thought I could control exactly how many calories I was consuming just by looking at the packaging. What I didn't realise was that by eating scientifically and obsessing over the numbers, I was becoming more and more disconnected from where my food actually came from. I saw food as a 'thing' – a commodity I needed to control.

My dad was always a keen gardener and, a few years ago, I spent an afternoon with him picking cherries and plums and blackberries off trees and bushes in his back garden and digging up carrots and potatoes from his vegetable patch. When I got home, I prepared them without a second thought about calories or nutrients or how healthy or 'clean' each ingredient was. Instead, I was thinking about what meal I could create, how to cook the vegetables, and what to eat them with. All of a sudden, I began to appreciate food in a way I'd never done before and it reduced my fear and anxiety around it. I made an effort to shop at farmers' markets and meet the people who actually produced my food, and I planted my own strawberries in a tub on my balcony.

Our connection to nature is associated with better overall well-being. And when we see food as less of an object for consumption and more of a relationship between sunlight, soil, grower, cook and eater, we don't need to worry about nutrients or health claims.

Fresh loganberries from my Dad's garden.

Why We Worry About What We Eat

There are three main reasons why we might worry about what we eat: fear of getting fat, fear of getting sick and fear of being judged.

FEAR OF WEIGHT GAIN

Often our worries about what we eat are strongly linked with our fear of getting fat. The drive for thinness is so prevalent in our culture that psychologists have come up with several labels relating to it: procrescophobia (fear of gaining weight), obesophobia (fear of getting obese) and gravitophobia (fear of stepping on the scales). Looking back, one of the main reasons I dieted to begin with was because I was scared of getting fat. And this is no surprise in a society that promotes thinness as successful and fatness as shameful. Whether it's making us gain weight, get acne or become bloated, food is increasingly being associated in the media with something that can do terrible things to the way we look.

FOOD, WEIGHT AND BODY IMAGE

Dieting is often marketed as a one-way ticket to love your body. In reality, going on a diet is not necessarily going to improve how you feel about your body. Research has found that, as well as the frequency of dieting being associated with weight gain, dieting more often is also linked with body dissatisfaction and low self-esteem. In a study looking at the impact of dieting on body image, researchers found that the more people dieted, the unhappier they were likely to be with their body and the more insecure they felt. Despite the diet industry trying to persuade us that cutting out food groups and counting calories will lead us to health, happiness and confidence in our own skin, research shows that excessive dieting does just the opposite – it can lead to poor body image, reduce our self-worth and cause depression.

Unless your weight is risking your health (in which case I recommend seeking professional help), it is far more effective to build a fear-free relationship with food before turning your attention to your weight. Your weight tends to take care of itself once you escape a diet mentality (and the repetitive cycle of self-deprivation, emotional eating, yo-yoing weight and poor body image that often comes with it). Emerging research into intuitive eating suggests that when people value their internal cues for hunger and fullness (known as interoceptive awareness) and trust them by eating accordingly (known as interoceptive responsiveness) they have a healthier Body Mass Index (BMI), are happier with their weight and body, feel greater body appreciation and life satisfaction, are more self-accepting, and are more likely to exercise (because they enjoy being active!).

When you begin to respect your body rather than criticise it, it is far easier to identify when you are hungry and when you are full, and then eat according to what your body needs to reach or maintain a healthy weight.

Although food, weight and body image are intimately linked, there are many benefits of fear-free eating that have nothing to do with weight. You can have a healthy relationship with food even if you're not the weight you'd like to be and you don't love every part of your body. Developing a fear-free relationship with food and not feeling 100 per cent happy with your body 100 per cent of the time is okay.

If you do find that once you have built a healthier relationship with food, you still want to change your weight or shape, you will be able to approach it in a much healthier and more caring way – one that focuses on nourishment rather than deprivation and uses self-love instead of self-control. It is perfectly possible to remove all dietary restrictions while improving your health and reaching a weight you are happy with.

FEAR OF GETTING SICK

As well as concerns about weight gain, one of the worries perpetuating my own fear of certain foods, like sugar and gluten, was getting sick. For example, as I became consumed by the Paleo diet culture (a diet based on what some people assume our ancient ancestors ate, which includes banning entire food groups such as grains and legumes), I believed the myths and exaggerated claims that sugar, specifically fructose, was toxic. I read on popular Paleo blogs that fructose could cause everything from digestive distress to high blood pressure, so I attempted to eliminate it completely from my diet – even cutting out fruit. It seems absurd when I look back to think I restricted something as natural and nourishing as fruit because 'experts' promoting a pseudoscientific diet trend recommended it.

Both nutrition scientists and the media play a huge role in frightening us about the health consequences of certain foods that only really concern a minority. Of course there are some diseases where changing

your diet can help you manage the condition (and changing your diet is essential for conditions such as diabetes and coeliac disease), but there is a big difference between disease management and disease prevention when it comes to our food choices. Our anxiety is perpetuated because nutrition advice changes so often. In the 1980s we were advised to swap butter for margarine because it contained less saturated fat. However, experts are now recommending that we return to butter because it turns out that saturated fat isn't that bad after all and the trans fat in margarine is far more dangerous for our health. In addition, for decades we were told to limit our egg consumption because they are high in cholesterol (which was thought to increase the risk of heart disease). Now experts have removed these recommendations because evidence has shown that healthy people who eat eggs don't have an increased risk of heart disease after all!

Examples such as these are one of the main reasons I have included a section on nutrition (Part 2, pages 55–69) in the book to dispel any nutrition-related health information that has been misreported by the media or exaggerated in wellness books and blogs.

FEAR OF BEING JUDGED

The third reason many of us worry about what we eat is that we fear being judged. The pressure to conform to certain diets or nutrition trends has been heightened by the use of social media, specifically Instagram, to share our food choices. I use Instagram (@NicolaJaneHobbs) – it's a great way to connect with other people and build a community – but I used to worry about sharing recipes that contained ingredients some people may judge as 'bad' or 'unhealthy', such as gluten or dairy, for fear of criticism. I've found that now I have a relationship with food that is guided by freedom instead of fear, I worry far less about other people's judgements of what I eat and I don't feel the pressure to conform to whatever food trend is popular at the time.

SOCIAL MEDIA AND OUR RELATIONSHIP WITH FOOD

Ninety per cent of 16- to 34-year-olds use social media, so it is important to understand the effect it has on our well-being. In particular, Instagram's healthy eating community has recently grown rapidly, with over 80 million pictures using the #eatclean or #cleaneating hashtags; over 50 million using the #healthyeating or #healthyfood hashtags; and another 40 million photos tagged with #diet.

This healthy eating movement has had a great positive impact on health by encouraging us to eat more vegetables and inspiring us to explore new foods, but there is concern among health professionals that it can encourage psychological problems around food, exercise and body image. One concern is the extreme attitudes to eating and exercise that often accompany the popular healthy eating hashtags – it seems that social media has become a socially acceptable way of rationalising extreme diets, dysfunctional eating and over-exercising.

Another concern is that some social media influencers who have a large following encourage their followers to restrict their diets by cutting out food groups without having any professional training or scientific evidence behind their advice. While most of these influencers have good intentions, if you are making people anxious and paranoid about eating, then you are doing more harm than good.

A final concern is that we tend to follow those who share beliefs that are similar to our own. This can lead us to believing that an extreme diet or a specific body shape is healthier and more normal than it actually is. This can cause us to feel increased pressure to follow a certain diet or look a certain way. For example, I used to follow a lot of Paleo accounts on Instagram to get recipe inspiration, but I found I was feeling increasingly guilty if I ate anything that wasn't classed as Paleo, such as rice, beans, bread and yogurt, even though these foods made me feel good. By unfollowing any Instagram accounts promoting a restrictive Paleo diet, I stopped comparing my food choices to other people in the Paleo community, which then allowed me to eat what I felt was right for my body instead of conforming to someone else's food rules.

I'm not suggesting you should remove yourself from social media entirely. In fact, it can be an incredibly informative, inspiring and supportive community. What I am suggesting is that you reflect on the impact it has on your life – both positive and negative. If you find scrolling through Instagram makes you feel guilty about your food choices, insecure about your body, and just generally leaves you feeling disheartened, then simply unfollow any accounts that leave you feeling this way and seek out other role models that inspire you.

Fear-Based Eating Versus Fear-Free Eating

One of the reasons I prefer to use the phrase 'fear-based eating' as opposed to 'disordered eating' is because I believe it is destructive to call anyone disordered and the opposite of disordered eating is ordered eating – and it is very difficult to define what that is. Likewise, I prefer to use the phrase 'fear-free eating' instead of 'healthy eating' because views on what a 'healthy' diet is, even by professionals, vary considerably.

The overriding aim of *Fear-Free Food* is to give you the tools and the confidence to move away from fear-based eating and towards fear-free eating.

FEAR-BASED EATING

Fear-based eating doesn't mean you have an eating disorder or that there's anything wrong with you; it just means you've absorbed unhelpful habits and attitudes around eating from society instead of trusting your body.

It's often difficult to find loopholes in your own relationship with food until you know what to look for so see if you can relate to any of the following fear-based thoughts, feelings and behaviours:

I beat myself up when I don't see the results I expect and deny myself pleasure until I have what I feel is the 'perfect' body.

I have rules that determine what I can and can't eat and sometimes cut out entire food groups (for example, carbs).

I feel my diet is harsh and restrictive and often find myself 'starting again on Monday' because I 'fall off the bandwagon'.

I find it difficult to make spontaneous decisions around food and get anxious if the supermarket doesn't have the regular brands I buy.

I like to weigh everything I eat, control the calories in my meals or track how much protein, fat and carbs there are in my food.

I spend a lot of time researching nutrition and talking about food and often prioritise food (and exercise) which means missing out on other things in life, such as socialising with friends.

I divide foods into 'good' and 'bad' or 'healthy' and 'unhealthy', and feel guilty if I eat anything 'bad', 'not clean' or 'unhealthy'.

I feel like everything to do with food is a big deal and I find myself thinking about food a lot of the time.

These fear-based thoughts, feelings and habits are usually not obvious at the time. So, use the statements opposite to take a more objective view of your eating mentality and behaviours and how fear-based eating may be harming your health and happiness. Once you are aware of the negative effects dieting and fear-based eating are having on your life, it is easier to begin letting go of this mentality and moving towards a fear-free way of eating.

One challenge that many of my clients face in becoming more aware of their fear-based eating is that dieting, and the rules and restrictions that come with it, has become so pervasive in our culture they're almost invisible. They can hide under the guise of many popular diet and lifestyle trends, including:

CLEAN EATING
This term began with good intentions: it implied we should eat natural wholefoods, such as fruit, vegetables, wholegrains and beans, avoid processed and packaged foods, and cook from scratch. Unfortunately, the phrase implies that if we don't 'eat clean' then what we eat is dirty and, by default, we are lazy and being careless with our diet and life. It demonises certain foods and the food it does recommend (such as organic vegetables, grass-fed meat and cold-pressed juice) is often expensive and beyond the reach of what most of us can afford. The anxiety clean eating can foster around our food choices often revolves around restricting one or more food groups (including sugar, gluten, dairy and soya) without any real scientific evidence. Rather than inspiring readers to nourish themselves better, a study looking at the content of clean-eating blogs found that many bloggers were actually promoting ideas related to disordered eating and fat stigmatisation and often shared messages that were likely to induce guilt in their readers.

VEGETARIAN AND VEGAN
Many people avoid animal products for ethical and environmental reasons and this is in no way unhealthy. What is unhealthy is when we cut out whole food groups like meat and dairy out of unnecessary *anxiety*. Some books and blogs promoting a vegan diet misrepresent scientific evidence about the health benefits of veganism and dangers of meat which can leave us feeling confused and scared about health risks that are only really an issue for a minority of the population. Restricting our consumption of animal food under the label of 'vegan' or 'vegetarian' can be one way we let anxiety around food restrict our lives. I was a vegetarian as a child but I decided to reintroduce meat into my diet when I was 19 to see how it made me feel. After a year or two of experimenting with including meat in my meals, I decided not to continue eating it – not out of guilt or anxiety but because I found eating it left me feeling sleepy and sluggish instead of healthy and energised.

PALEO AND KETOGENIC
I have grouped Paleo and ketogenic diets together to highlight how easy it is to become confused and anxious around food when you look at the contradictory rules and restrictions surrounding diets. For example, the Paleo diet (a diet based on the types of food presumed to have been eaten by Paleolithic humans at least 2 million years ago) promotes eating meat, fish and vegetables such as greens and sweet potatoes, and excluding dairy, grains and processed foods. The ketogenic diet (a very low-carb and high-fat diet designed to get the body into a metabolic state called 'ketosis') promotes eating high-fat dairy, such as butter and cheese, and avoiding high-carb vegetables, such as sweet potatoes – opposite to what is recommended by the Paleo diet.

There are, of course, many other diets out there that are based on restricting certain food groups such as low-carb, 5:2, acid-alkaline, high-protein, or IIFYM (if it fits your macros). Whatever the restriction, whether a pre-existing unhealthy relationship with food makes these diets more appealing to you or following one of these diets has caused your unhealthy relationship with food is not important. What *is* important is understanding whether following these diets is having a negative impact on your life. If it is, the only way to heal your relationship with food is to stop the diet.

It's worth mentioning that in some cases, calorie counting, meal planning, and other strategies traditionally used in restrictive dieting can actually be helpful tools when used for a short period in order to become reacquainted with your body's biology and rebuild a healthy relationship with food. This is beyond the scope of this book but you can find out more about strategies to help you move from a fear-based to fear-free way of eating at www.FearFreeFood.co.uk.

FEAR-FREE EATING

Fear-free eating is eating in a way that will enhance your health and happiness. This means making food choices based on nutrition, pleasure, intuition, tradition and connection. It means eating deliberately – from a place of freedom instead of fear.

Look at the thoughts and feelings listed below and notice the ways in which you could relate to food with a kinder, gentler, more nourishing mentality that comes with fear-free eating:

I eat in a healthful and self-loving way without self-imposed rules and restrictions.

I nourish myself without deprivation and eat in a way that supports how I want my body to feel.

I respect evidence-based nutrition information instead of food myths, exaggerated health claims and extreme diets.

I understand that not every ingredient has to have a nutritional purpose all the time and I enjoy eating a wide variety of foods and experimenting with new recipes.

I have let go of any unnecessary emotion around food such as fear, guilt and judgement. Eating a cupcake is emotionally equal to eating a banana.

I take responsibility for my food choices – not because I want to fit into a certain pair of jeans but because I love and respect my body enough to make food choices that make me feel healthy and energised.

I understand there is no right or wrong way to eat, that food does not exist on a dramatic spectrum of 'healthy' and 'unhealthy' and know that no food is 'bad' or 'toxic'.

I accept that everyone has different nutritional needs, different tastes and different metabolisms so there is no point comparing my diet to anyone else's.

I forgive myself for any past dieting and not treating my body with love and kindness sooner.

I make time to eat and make sure I eat enough.

Compare these thoughts and feelings with those on page 32 and notice whether you are eating more from a place of fear and restriction or nourishment and freedom.

As you read through this book and reflect on your relationship with food, you will develop your own definition of what fear-free eating means to you.

FOR ME, FEAR-FREE EATING MEANS...

... eating foods that I enjoy and that bring me pleasure.

... eating in a way that allows me to meet all my nutritional needs and maintain a healthy weight, and leaves me feeling healthy and energised.

... accepting that I don't have a perfect diet (and no one else does either): I eat wholefoods most of the time because they make me feel amazing, but I also eat processed foods when it is practical and if they taste good.

... I eat when I'm hungry and stop when I'm full for the majority of the time, but I might eat a little more if I'm really enjoying what I'm eating or, if I'm busy, I might eat a little less.

... I am more mindful of my food choices sometimes but I never diet restrictively or take anything to the extreme.

How to Eat Freely

Understanding your current relationship with food and becoming aware of any diet-based rules, unhealthy habits and unhelpful attitudes and anxieties around eating is essential in rebuilding a healthy relationship with food. The tools you'll find on the next few pages will give you the six steps I used on my own journey and that I use with my clients to help them eat and live with more freedom. You'll also find extra tools to help you cope with cravings, understand overeating and make changing your eating habits a little bit easier.

I'd recommend getting a notebook and writing the answers down as it encourages you to really reflect on how you feel and it can be especially helpful to read back responses when they are written in your own handwriting. If you need more support, you can find additional fear-free eating tools and strategies at: www.FearFreeFood.co.uk.

One of the reasons I love having a fear-free relationship with food is so I can fully enjoy mealtimes with friends and family. Some of my favourite recipes to make when friends come over are Lentil Salad with Goat's Cheese and Walnuts (page 131) and Spicy Sweet Potato Wedges (page 168).

STEP 1: IDENTIFY HOW A FEAR-BASED RELATIONSHIP WITH FOOD IS HAVING A NEGATIVE IMPACT ON YOUR LIFE

In order to move from restriction to freedom when it comes to eating, it can be helpful to identify the specific beliefs you hold around food, any diet rules you have absorbed from society and how they are harming your physical, mental and emotional health. You may have picked up rules from extreme diets you've been on in the past, got sucked into exaggerated nutrition claims from the media or simply trusted pseudoscientific information you stumbled across on a healthy eating blog or social media account (it's okay – I've been there too!).

It's also helpful to think about any eating habits you have that you feel are limiting your life in some way – either in terms of your health and fitness or in the way they stop you doing the things you love (like going out for brunch with friends).

Answer the following questions (I have included the most common food rules and anxieties around eating my clients share with me which you may be able to relate to):

✪ Do you have any fear-based beliefs around food, restrictive eating habits or food rules? List them below:

For example:
- Believing foods are either healthy or unhealthy
- Counting calories, carbs, fat, or protein
- Avoiding certain foods or food groups (e.g. foods high in sugar, carbs and fat)
- Comparing what you eat to other people (in real life or online)
- Only eating 'safe' foods
- Eating at certain times of the day
- Exercising to compensate for what you have eaten.

✪ How is dieting and fear-based eating negatively affecting your health and life as a whole?

For example:

- Feeling tired all the time
- Feeling disconnected from your appetite (not knowing when you're hungry or full)
- Weight changes and lowered metabolism
- Body image anxiety
- Cravings for carbs and sugary foods
- Anxiety about eating out
- Feelings of guilt after eating or breaking food rules
- Lack of trust in your body
- Fear of not being able to stop eating certain foods once you start
- Preoccupation with food, dieting and weight
- Avoiding social situations involving food.

STEP 2: IDENTIFY WHY YOU WANT TO HAVE A FEAR-FREE RELATIONSHIP WITH FOOD

Dieting and food fads are so common in society that we see them as normal, even if the rules and restrictions that often accompany them end up causing unnecessary anxiety, impacting on our social life and reducing our overall quality of life. For example, when I was eating clean and

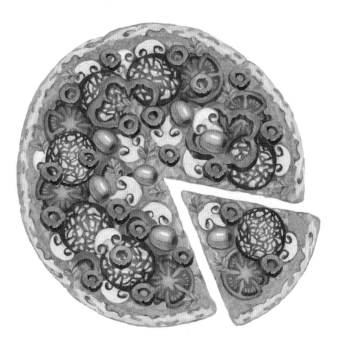

calorie counting, going out for dinner would cause disproportionate anxiety about what the restaurant served ('What oil is the food cooked in?', 'Is it organic?', 'How many calories does it contain?'), which took the enjoyment out of the whole experience. One of my reasons for walking away from dieting was so that I could go out to dinner with friends, choose whatever I fancied from the menu, and eat as much of it as I wanted without anxiety or guilt. Identifying this helped me stay motivated in rebuilding a healthy relationship with food even when relearning to eat without rules and beginning to trust my body felt a little scary.

Reflecting on your current relationship with food and becoming aware of why you would like to eat with less guilt and confusion and with greater confidence and freedom is key in building a fear-free relationship with food.

Ask yourself the following questions:

✪ Why do you want to have a fear-free relationship with food?

For example:
- To trust your body
- To feel more energised
- To not have food occupy your thoughts 24/7
- To eat ice cream without feeling guilty
- To experiment with new recipes
- To eat a greater variety of foods without anxiety
- To have more free time to spend with friends instead of researching nutrition.

✪ What new things could you do if you stopped dieting, let go of rules and restrictions around eating, and built a fear-free relationship with food?

For example:
- Enjoy spontaneous meals out with friends
- Host dinner parties
- Explore new restaurants with your partner
- Bake cupcakes with your kids.

STEP 3: GIVE UP THE DIET MENTALITY

A diet mentality is a mindset where your relationship with food is based around rules and restrictions. This can include meticulously counting calories, limiting fats or carbs, only eating 'safe' foods, comparing your food choices with other people's, and treating food as something that needs to be 'earnt'. And this attitude towards food is incredibly common: research suggests that over 50 per cent of people go on a diet every year (65 per cent of women and 44 per cent of men). Despite how common dieting is, emerging research suggests that it doesn't lead to any long-term improvements to health and repeated dieting may actually cause an increased risk of high blood pressure, diabetes, obesity and eating disorders, as well as creating a negative, guilt-based relationship with food. Dieting and guilt have a tendency to occur in tandem. And, when you give up the dieting mentality, eating with more enjoyment and less guilt tends to be a natural by-product.

When I was a slave to the diet culture, I just accepted that in order to stay slim and healthy I needed to constantly watch what I ate, control my appetite and restrict my food to 'healthy food' (according to my own made-up definition of what 'healthy food' comprised). Even though it felt far from natural, I thought this kind of restrictive dieting was normal and necessary.

As my perspective on eating started to shift and I decided to build a healthier relationship with food, I realised that there was no way I could let go of guilt and anxiety around food and create more freedom and enjoyment around eating while still dieting. So I had to give it up. And once I did give up the dieting mentality, I learned that I could eat more, enjoy dessert regularly and still stay healthy, feel strong and energised, and maintain a healthy weight.

In the same way that fear-free eating as a whole is not about extreme indulgence, giving up the dieting mentality is not about giving up nutritious foods and eating with complete disregard for health. Instead it's about eating in a way that feels natural and liberating instead of harsh and restrictive. In fact, non-dieters who are attuned to their appetite tend to balance what they eat quite naturally – enjoying mostly nutritious foods with just a little 'play food' (low-nutrient food eaten for fun and pleasure) when they fancy it.

Dieting is often used as a way to cope with life and the thought of giving it up can be terrifying (especially when it feels like the rest of the world is on a diet!). But it is worth considering the impact having a dieting mentality may be having on your life and what life would be like without it. Note down your thoughts to the questions below:

✪ Reflect on whether you have a diet mentality. What dieting attitudes do you have? How might these attitudes be creating or maintaining a fear-based relationship with food?

For example, common diet mentality beliefs I hear when clients first come to me include: willpower is needed to be healthy; clean eating represents self-control; food choices are a reflection of morality and self-worth.

✪ How could you reframe each belief stemming from a diet mentality with an alternative that empowers you to nourish and care for yourself?

For example, you could replace the belief, "If I don't diet, I will lose control" with the kinder alternative, "If I don't diet, I can learn how to trust my body, respect my appetite, and nourish myself properly."

✪ What dieting tools can you get rid of to help you let go of the dieting mentality and prevent yourself getting sucked back in?

For example, throwing away diet books; deleting calorie counting apps from your phone; not participating in conversations about dieting; unfollowing anyone on social media who promotes dieting.

STEP 4: PRACTISE THE PAUSE

Often the diet rules we've absorbed from society and the beliefs we have around food are so automatic that we don't even realise the anxiety this diet mentality is producing. Identifying these fear-based food beliefs and rules in Steps 1, 2 and 3 (pages 36–38) will have helped you become more aware of them so practising the pause is the next step to letting go of these anxieties and restrictions.

What does practising the pause actually mean? Well, just that – briefly stopping before cooking or eating so you can eat from intention instead of from habit. In doing so, you can consciously unlink food from diet-based rules, dismiss any unnecessary, but often automatic, guilt and instead choose to cook and eat foods that will truly nourish you. Pausing in this way not only short circuits the mental patterns that cause anxiety but also brings you into the present moment so you can tune into your body and eat more mindfully. Mindfulness is about paying attention to the present moment and being aware of any thoughts, emotions and physical sensations without judgement. This empowers you to free yourself from any unhealthy habits and thought patterns, including unhealthy eating habits and anxieties surrounding food. By eating mindfully, you begin respecting your own inner wisdom to choose foods to eat that are both enjoyable and nourishing, trust hunger and fullness cues to tell you when to start and stop eating, and embrace preparing, cooking and eating food as opportunities for self-care and nourishment.

As I was moving away from dieting and clean eating, I found that when I paused for a moment, took a couple of deep breaths and tuned into my thoughts and feelings, it gave me space to notice the faulty beliefs and anxieties I had around food. I could then choose not to allow those anxieties to control my food choices. Instead, I gave myself permission to eat what I wanted in a way that would really nourish me.

For example, my carb phobia and mistaken beliefs around gluten damaging my gut meant that replacing spaghetti with 'courgetti' and rice with 'cauliflower rice' (grated cauliflower) had become normal and habitual for me. Practising the pause before I chose what I was going to serve with my lentil dhal for dinner meant that I could begin to dismiss my anxieties around carbs. Instead of having cauliflower rice out of anxiety and habit, I could make a mindful and conscious choice to serve my dhal with pilau rice because that is what I really enjoyed eating, and it would give me the energy and nourishment I needed. (There is a delicious Coconut and Aubergine Dhal recipe on page 161!)

Practise pausing each time you choose something to eat and become aware of any food beliefs, rules or anxieties that pop into your head – no matter how small. Make a note of them and gradually start to dismiss them by making deliberate food choices that will leave you feeling healthier and happier. To get you started, below I've included a few examples of common faulty food beliefs and self-imposed eating rules that my clients often notice they have absorbed from our diet culture when they practise the pause. (I explain why they are faulty in 'Fear-Free Nutrition', pages 57, 60 and 62.)

- ✪ 'Eating carbs will make me fat.'
- ✪ 'Gluten-free food is healthier than food containing gluten.'
- ✪ 'I need to cut out all processed foods in order to be healthy.'
- ✪ 'Fruit isn't healthy because it has a lot of sugar in it.'
- ✪ 'Fat-free foods are healthier than full-fat versions.'
- ✪ 'White potatoes are unhealthy.'
- ✪ 'Eating after 6 p.m. will make me gain weight.'

STEP 5: LEARN TO TRUST YOUR BODY

Millions of us have dieted all our lives. We've absorbed unhealthy attitudes around food from society and our sense of hunger is often skewed by years of fad diets or comfort eating. This means that many of us are no longer in tune with our appetite and struggle to eat when we're hungry and stop when we're full.

Fear-free eating is largely about reigniting trust in your body and your appetite. This involves:

- ✪ Unlinking food from diet-based rules.
- ✪ Eating intuitively and mindfully.
- ✪ Giving yourself permission to nourish yourself.
- ✪ Eating *mainly* for physical rather than emotional reasons.
- ✪ Balancing nutrition with pleasure.
- ✪ Eating foods that you like eating, make you feel good and energise your body.
- ✪ Relying on your hunger and fullness cues to decide what, when and how much to eat.

Research suggests that the more trust we have in our body, the less likely we are to go on restrictive diets, engage in extreme weight loss behaviour or binge eat. Also, our Body Mass Index (BMI) is likely to be healthier.

Becoming aware of any mistrust you have in your body can be helpful in rebuilding it. Here's a list of things my clients have shared which reflects the lack of trust they had in their body when trapped in a dieting mentality – you might be able to relate to some of them:

- ✪ 'I'm worried that if I eat one biscuit I'll end up eating the whole packet.'
- ✪ 'I often fancy a jacket potato for lunch but only have salads because I'm scared eating carbs will make me fat.'
- ✪ 'I make sure my lunch is always under 350 calories even though it never fills me up.'
- ✪ 'If I eat a big breakfast then I'll skip lunch even if I'm hungry.'
- ✪ 'I don't keep ice cream in the house because I can't trust myself not to eat it all.'

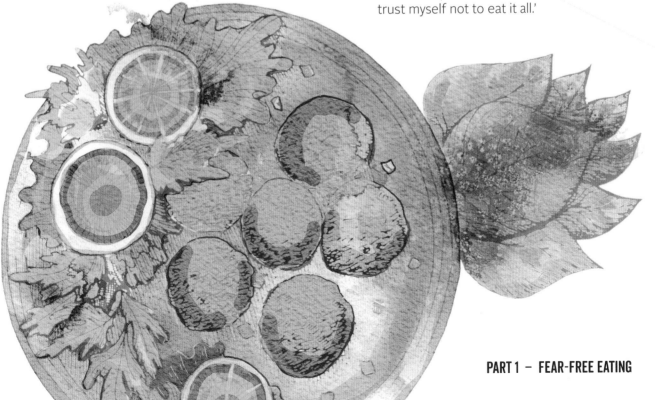

TRUST YOUR APPETITE

Fear-free eating, intuitive eating, mindful eating, natural eating, non-diet eating, and eating competence are all part of a new anti-diet paradigm which rejects the idea that we have to follow rule-based diets and consciously control our food intake because our bodies can't be trusted. Instead, these approaches encourage you to become more in tune with your appetite, honour your homeostatic hunger signals (the signals your body naturally sends out to stay in balance) and learn to trust your body again.

Research into non-diet eating shows that you can remove all the rules and restrictions around food and still be healthy. Studies have found associations between non-diet eating and reduced cholesterol and blood pressure, increased self-esteem and body satisfaction, and improved physical fitness. Non-diet eating has also been linked with:

✪ increased fruit and vegetable intake;
✪ better overall nutrition due to more dietary variety;
✪ reduced emotional eating and binge eating;
✪ fewer food cravings;
✪ lower BMI;
✪ better stress management;
✪ reduced depression and anxiety;
✪ better overall well-being.

TRACKING HUNGER AND FULLNESS

If you have dieted for years, then it can take time to rebuild trust in your appetite. The sensations of hunger and fullness are highly individual so a helpful way of getting in touch with your body is using the Hunger–Fullness Scale. This helps to quantify your hunger on a scale of -10 to 10 (where -10 is 'empty' and 10 is 'stuffed to bursting') so you can begin to learn what healthy hunger feels like and how much and how often you need to eat to feel satisfied and energised.

10	feeling physically sick, stuffed to bursting
9	
8	physically uncomfortable, stomach ache
7	
6	very full
5	
4	pleasantly satisfied, gentle fullness
3	
2	getting full, feel the need to eat more to be satisfied
1	
0	neutral, not hungry or full
-1	
-2	occasional gurgling
-3	
-4	gentle stomach rumbling, thoughts about eating
-5	
-6	loud stomach growling, difficulty concentrating
-7	
-8	ravenous, stomach ache
-9	
-10	empty, weak, light-headed

Experiment using this scale to track your levels of hunger and satiety over the course of the day, especially around meal times. This may feel hyperconscious to begin with so treat the Hunger–Fullness Scale as a tool; as you tune back into your body's signals, eating in accordance with your body's biology will happen quite naturally.

As you do this, remember that hunger is not the enemy, nor is it an emergency. Tracking the intensity of your hunger will help you to understand what healthy hunger feels like – and this may take a bit of time (especially if you have been numbing out your hunger for years).

Learning what healthy hunger felt like took me a little practice. At first, I thought the tiniest bit of hunger (a rating of -2) meant I needed to eat immediately, when actually it's okay to be a little bit hungry. Equally, sometimes I waited until my hunger was a rating of -8 or -9 and I learned that if I left it that long, I became anxious around eating and was more likely to overeat.

The same is true for learning what a comfortable level of fullness feels like. This took me a little while to learn too – sometimes I only ate until a rating of 3 and I would be hungry again an hour later, and other times I ate until a rating of 8 and felt like I needed a nap!

A dieting mentality often means taking things to the extreme. In the same way you often numb out healthy hunger signals when you're on a diet and wait until you're ravenous before eating, you may also find that you numb out healthy fullness signals too and end up eating far more than what you really needed to feel satisfied. Being comfortably full doesn't mean feeling stuffed after a meal. It means finishing a meal so you feel better than when you started, have energy and focus, and can get on with your day without thinking about food until your next meal.

Ayurveda, one of the world's oldest medical systems originating in India over 5000 years ago, recommends eating until we feel 75 per cent full. And the Okinawans (one of the Blue Zones populations, see page 22) have a practice called 'Hara Hachi Bu', which means eating until you're 80 per cent full. It can take a little while to get to know what a healthy level of fullness feels like so tracking your satiety levels can help you become more in tune with how much and how often you need to eat to feel good.

It's also helpful to become aware of how eating different types of food makes you feel in terms of your hunger and fullness. Many dieters attempt to 'trick' their body into feeling full by eating low-energy, high-volume foods such as salad, egg whites, popcorn, and rice cakes, or by drinking calorie-free diet sodas and black coffee to get the sensation of fullness. Although these diet tricks may help you feel full on an hour-by-hour basis, it's difficult to outsmart biology long term. My clients often report that when they used to eat like this, the lack of energy and nutrients in these diet foods and drinks would catch up with them. They noticed that after a day or so of filling up on low-energy 'diet foods', their hunger would increase to a point where they were more likely to overeat and binge – a normal and natural response to energy restriction (and NOT due to a lack of willpower).

Understanding your appetite, trusting your body and eating intuitively is something that you will refine over your lifetime so treat this as an exploration. If you struggle to start with and find you eat too much or not enough, or you leave it too long between meals, don't worry – there's always the next time.

And although fear-free eating means you want to eat based on your hunger and fullness most of the time, it doesn't mean you can never eat when you're not hungry. If I've just eaten lunch and am pretty full up but a friend pops over with freshly baked cookies, I sure as hell am going to have one!

It's worth noting that if you are struggling with an eating disorder such as anorexia nervosa or bulimia nervosa, then your hunger and fullness signals may not be reliable until you are a healthy weight. If this is the case, I would recommend speaking to a professional who can help you.

STEP 6: GIVE YOURSELF UNCONDITIONAL FREEDOM TO EAT

If you have dieted on and off for most of your life, you'll know that it doesn't bring you the health and happiness you're looking for. And that's because dieting is an unnatural way of eating. In contrast, non-diet eating is an innate instinct. Children eat what they like, when they are hungry and until they are full, which shows us how we are all programmed to eat intuitively from birth. However, aspects of our environment, such as food adverts, nutrition trends and the diet culture as a whole, potentially in combination with years of calorie counting, weight watching and restrictive dieting, can mean we lose touch with our internal signals for hunger and fullness. Tracking your appetite using the tools in Step 5 (page 41–43) will help you learn to trust your body. The next step is giving yourself permission to eat so you can respond to your body's signals and make peace with food.

Giving yourself permission to eat means eating as much as you are hungry for until you are satisfied. It means eating what you want and feeling good about eating. It means going to a meal hungry and paying attention to the tastes and textures and how the food makes your body feel. It means you eat a huge variety of food and take nutrition into account when making food choices without obsessing over it. It means you eat nutritious foods because you enjoy them and not because you feel you 'should'. It means sometimes overeating and sometimes undereating, but trusting that you'll never take anything to the extreme because you have faith in your body to keep you in balance.

A common fear my clients express (which I also experienced when I was moving to a fear-free way of eating) is that giving themselves permission to eat whatever they want means they will binge on all the foods they had previously forbidden themselves from eating. However, emerging research on binge eating suggests that eating these 'forbidden foods' as part of a balanced way of eating may actually reduce the likelihood of overeating them. After I learnt that giving myself permission to eat what I really wanted didn't mean I would binge on previously 'forbidden foods', I found it incredibly liberating to escape the rules and restrictions of a diet mentality. My clients often report how empowering it feels to trust, respect and nourish their body (regardless of how they feel about its weight or shape) by allowing all foods into their eating world and giving themselves unconditional permission to eat.

It can feel scary to let go of the rules and rigidity of dieting when you give yourself permission to eat, so use the following three tools to help you:

1. FEED YOUR INNER CHILD

In order to move away from the rules of the diet industry and eat the foods that your body is signalling for, it can be helpful to reflect on what you used to enjoy eating as a child before the diet industry told you what to eat. As a kid some of my favourites were pasta, cherry tomatoes, cucumber sticks, my Nan's pancakes with a sprinkling of brown sugar, satsumas, peanut butter on toast, jacket potatoes with steaming hot beans, and all kinds of yogurt! Answer the following questions:

- What did you eat as a child (before you ever dieted)?
- What were your favourite foods?
- What foods made you feel energised?
- What kind of feelings did you have around food (for example, excitement at going out for a picnic)?
- How did you make food fun (for example, decorating cakes or making smoothies)?

2. FIND YOUR NATURAL RHYTHM

At first glance, giving yourself unconditional permission to eat and trusting your body may make eating seem erratic, impulsive and unpredictable, especially if you've spent years abiding by food rules or following some kind of meal plan or eating structure.

But, just because fear-free eating doesn't have the structure of calorie counts or meal plans, it doesn't mean that your appetite is totally unpredictable. All that happens is that, instead of following a structure that is created externally by diet plans, clean eating guides or messages in your head telling you what you should and shouldn't eat, you begin respecting the structure that is created internally by your body. What I have found as I have moved towards a fear-free way of eating is that my body has a natural structure: I'm hungry at similar times each day; I feel good eating specific foods at certain times throughout the day; and I am naturally drawn towards foods and meals that make me feel my best. I still have structure – only it comes from my body rather than a meal plan or diet book. I have found my natural rhythm.

When you shift to eating according to your natural rhythm rather than an external structure, it gives you far greater flexibility and freedom with your eating. I used to freak out if I was going away on holiday and didn't know how to track my calories or measure my portions. But now I have trust in my body – I relax and enjoy an ice cream on the beach if I fancy one because I know that, even if I do overindulge a little while I'm away, my body's natural wisdom will keep me in balance.

This shift towards using an internal structure and trusting your inner wisdom to guide your food choices can be scary. To start with, as you go through a food-freeing phase, you might find it helpful to structure in regular mealtimes. Then, as you become more in tune with your appetite, discover what foods make you feel good and learn your natural rhythm, you'll find that intuitive eating falls into place quite naturally.

Keeping the following questions in mind as you learn to listen to the messages your body is giving you will help you find your natural rhythm. You might not know the answers right now, especially if you have dieted and overridden your natural instincts for a long time, but use them as tools as you reconnect to your body and tune into the clues it is giving you:

✪ How long after waking up do I feel hungry?
✪ What kind of foods do I feel good eating for breakfast?
✪ When does my stomach begin to rumble for lunch?
✪ What kind of foods do I feel good eating for lunch?
✪ Do I feel good having mid-morning and mid-afternoon snacks?
✪ What food leaves me feeling energised and would be easy to snack on?
✪ What time do I feel good eating dinner?
✪ What kind of foods do I feel good eating for dinner?
✪ How long do I need to wait before going to bed after my last meal or snack so I sleep well?
✪ What foods leave me feeling energised and which ones make me feel sluggish?

3. CREATE A LIST OF DAILY NON-NEGOTIABLES

Plunging straight into non-dieting after years of dieting can leave you feeling a little lost. It's helpful to create a list of things to do every day to help you tap into your hunger and fullness cues, ensure you're nourishing yourself well and check that you're supporting your transition to fear-free eating. This can include any routines, behaviours or habits relating to food or your life as a whole that will help you become healthier and happier.

Make a list of your daily non-negotiables – things that you will absolutely aim to do on a day-to-day basis – focusing on things to add to your day rather than things to avoid or restrict. I've shared some of my daily non-negotiables to get you started:

✪ Meditating for five to 10 minutes.
✪ Getting fresh air and spending time in nature.
✪ Basing most meals around as many colourful fruit and vegetables as possible.
✪ Getting at least seven hours' sleep a night.

Extra Tools for Fear-Free Eating

Breaking away from a dieting mentality, especially if you've had an unhealthy relationship with food for a long time, can throw up some challenges. The next few tools will help you to cope with the most common issues clients moving to a fear-free way of eating struggle with.

RELAX ABOUT UNDEREATING AND OVEREATING

We all undereat and overeat at times. Sometimes because of practicality, sometimes because of pleasure, and sometimes it's simply part of the process of learning to trust your body.

Schedules don't always allow for eating when your hunger peaks so, if you have a busy morning of back-to-back meetings, you might choose to eat a little more for breakfast because you know you won't be able to eat again until well into the afternoon. Likewise, you might end up undereating one day because of some event that is out of your control, such as a family emergency. Equally, you might eat a little past your usual point of fullness if you go out to dinner simply because you are having a good time and are really enjoying the food.

If you are in tune with your body, you'll notice that if you overeat at one meal, you probably won't feel as hungry at the next mealtime. Or if you undereat one day, the next day you'll feel hungrier than usual. These signals to eat a little more or a little less are your body's way of trying to stay in balance (homeostasis). And research indicates that it is quite normal for food intake to vary from day to day by 20–30 per cent (in terms of calories consumed – see page 56) with little change to bodyweight. This is because the body doesn't reset every 24 hours. When you undereat or overeat, your body will self-regulate by increasing or decreasing hunger over the period of a few days, weeks, or even over a few months to get back into balance. This is not the same as consciously restricting your food after a big meal out, but instead it's about becoming more aware of what your body is telling you and nourishing yourself appropriately.

And, if you do choose to overeat, eat with no strings attached (no skipping meals or doing an extra run the next day to compensate). Own that choice, have trust in your body's ability to maintain balance and get on with your life.

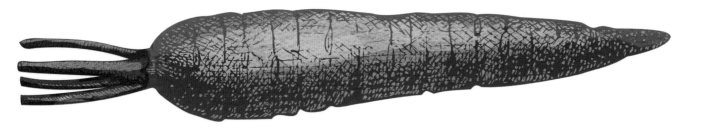

Whenever you feel like you have undereaten or overeaten, think about the following questions to understand why you have eaten more or less than your body needs and how your body responds in order to stay in balance:

✪ Why did I undereat or overeat?

For example, this may be for practical reasons such as having a busy day so you skipped lunch, or emotional reasons such as using food for comfort, or eating out of boredom.

✪ If I undereat or overate for emotional reasons, what was I feeling? How can I cope with these emotions without using food?

For example, it's quite common for my clients to notice they overeat when they are feeling lonely. By spending more time with friends, their overeating naturally reduces. Equally, some clients skip meals and undereat when they are experiencing stress because elements of their life feel out of control. By taking time out to reduce their stress levels, they then feel able to nourish themselves properly.

✪ What practical steps can I put in place to help me tune into my body's biological drive to rebalance if I have undereaten or overeaten?

For example, it's helpful to make sure you have a variety of nourishing foods to hand so you can feed your body what it is signalling for. It's also helpful to schedule in enough time to cook from scratch, eat with friends and family, and make sure you give yourself enough time to eat mindfully and savour your meals.

LEARN TO COPE WITH CRAVINGS

Craving cookies doesn't mean you are weak – it means you are human. Food cravings are very common (about 90 per cent of us experience them) and are not something we need to fear. These cravings are just part of life and we have a choice over how we respond to them.

For example, when I crave cookies, I get to decide how many cookies to eat, not to eat any cookies at all or to eat something more nutrient-rich instead of cookies (like an apple). These choices depend on my appetite, the social situation and how I'm feeling at the time. If I decide to eat a few cookies, then I enjoy them. And if I decide not to eat any cookies at all, then I don't feel deprived because I know there will always be another opportunity to eat them.

When you experience a powerful food craving ask yourself the following questions:

✪ Am I physically hungry?
✪ If I choose to eat what I'm craving, why would I be eating it (pleasure, connection, boredom, habit...) and how will it enhance my health and happiness?

The same is true for 'food addictions'. For a long time I thought I was addicted to sugar (partly because the media told me I was) so I cut it out of my diet. Yes, some foods have an addictive effect on our brain, but even if you do feel you have an addiction to sugar or chocolate or coffee, the goal is to be able to reignite trust in yourself so that you can eat these foods in *moderation*. Moderation doesn't mean elimination – it simply means not taking things to the extreme. If there is a specific food you avoid because you feel you are addicted to it, use what you have learned in Steps 5 and 6 (pages 41–43 and 44–46) to rebuild trust in yourself around this food so that it no longer has a hold on you and you don't have to spend the rest of your life avoiding it.

STRESS REDUCTION AND SELF-CARE

It is natural to feel slightly uncomfortable when you begin changing your eating habits and stop dieting or start reintroducing 'forbidden foods'. And sometimes this discomfort can feel a little overwhelming. One of the reasons this anxiety can feel so overpowering is because you have a busy mind – maybe you are stressed or anxious or in a rush. When you reduce stress and calm your mind, you'll find that you have more mental space to detach from any anxieties around food or urges to overeat.

And in those moments when you do feel stressed, you can actually embrace it as a tool to connect to the physical sensations of your body which in turn can help you connect with the physical sensation of hunger and fullness (Step 5). Answer the following questions:

✪ Where in my body do I feel stress?
   For example, tight shoulders, clenched jaw, knot in your stomach...
✪ Does it feel pleasant, unpleasant, or neutral?
✪ What can I do to move towards a more pleasant feeling?
   For example, meditate or talk to a friend.

You may find you feel more stressed around mealtimes, especially if you have a history of chronic dieting. This can make making peace with food more challenging and can cause digestive discomfort so here are a few tips for reducing stress around eating:

✪ Distraction reduces connection so aim to eat at least one meal a day in a calm, distraction-free environment (no TV, social media, work etc.).
✪ Have a small list of nourishing meals and snacks you can fall back on in times of stress so you don't skip meals or fall back into destructive eating habits. You want these to give you all the nutrients your body needs and be quick and easy to prepare.

✪ If there is a specific food that is causing you stress (because of anxiety over the ingredients, fear it will make you gain weight, or worries you will binge on it) then begin to make peace with it by eating it a few times a week. Pick one 'fear food' or 'forbidden food' and decide where and when you will eat it. Notice how you feel before, during and after you eat it and, as you begin to eat this food on a regular basis, you'll notice that any extreme emotions (fear, stress, guilt, excitement...) will begin to fade until it no longer causes you stress or has control over you but is something you can continue to eat and enjoy without judgement.

Exhaustion will also interfere with building a healthy relationship with food. Therefore, self-care is crucial for both reducing stress and giving you the energy, courage and confidence to break unhealthy eating habits and rebuild healthier ones.

Note down some ways you can start caring for yourself more. I've included a few examples to get you started...

✪ Asking for help with household jobs.
✪ Making time for an afternoon nap at the weekend.
✪ Scheduling time to socialise with friends in person – not just on social media!
✪ Getting a massage.
✪ Swapping an intense exercise class for a gentle yoga session.
✪ Learning to meditate.
✪ Getting out for some fresh air at lunchtime.
✪ Getting up 10 minutes earlier to make time to have a nourishing breakfast.
✪ Setting aside 20 minutes a day to read.

Making Food Fun

Food can and should be fun. When I was clean eating and stuck in the dieting mentality, it made simple things like food shopping a label-checking mission and turned what should be enjoyable experiences, like eating out and sharing meals with friends, into sources of anxiety.

EATING WITH FRIENDS AND FAMILY

In our hectic lives, we often end up eating alone – at our desks at work, on the go in between meetings or in front of the TV at home. And our dietary habits and food restrictions can also alienate us from enjoying meals together. All of this means we are often missing out on meaningful time with our loved ones.

My fear-based relationship with food meant that I often found myself eating alone. But when I started letting go of the dieting mentality and began having friends over for dinner, going out for weekend brunches and joining my family for Sunday roasts, mealtimes became one of the happiest parts of my day!

Making food fun and creating memories with friends over sandwiches, scones and cake.

We're all busy and fitting in family meals can seem like a struggle. So, instead of treating eating together like another thing on your to-do list, see it as an opportunity to relax, catch up with those you love and have fun. It doesn't take much – by setting aside 30–60 minutes from your day to cook and eat together, not only do you get to talk, reflect and make memories with loved ones, your relationship with food changes; instead of it being a source of anxiety and guilt, it becomes one of connection.

If you've got out of the habit of sharing meals then here are a few ideas to use food as an opportunity to connect with others:

- Instead of eating in front of the TV, aim to eat together around the table as a family as often as possible. Take turns with who cooks and who does the washing-up.
- Create a 'lunch group' at work – instead of eating at your desk, arrange to meet colleagues in the cafeteria or a communal area. You'll eat more mindfully, get to know each other better and probably be far more productive for having a proper break when you get back to your desk in the afternoon.
- Arrange a weekly get-together with friends where you all bring a dish based on a theme or cuisine, such as pizza, Thai food or something a little more interesting, like farm-to-table. This will help you to get excited about food again by introducing you to new recipes and creating a social atmosphere around food.
- Get in the habit of inviting friends and family over for Sunday brunch or a Sunday roast. And if you don't feel like cooking, use it as a chance to explore local cafes and restaurants and enjoy spending time with those you love.

EATING OUT

Having a fear-based relationship with food can turn eating out – ordinarily an opportunity to experience new foods and share a meal with friends and family – into a source of anxiety.

When I was stuck in a dieting mentality, I often turned down social occasions because they involved going to a restaurant. My anxieties over not knowing what was on the menu in advance, not knowing the nutritional content of my meal and not knowing how it was being cooked or if it contained gluten or dairy, or whatever food I was restricting at the time, meant I missed out on time with those I cared about. And, if I did eat out, I would end up stressing so much about the food that I missed out on all the benefits that came with it – trying new dishes, connecting with friends and not having to do the washing-up!

Eating out highlights the power of food beyond the nutrients it contains. We aren't just feeding or fuelling our body as if it is a machine – we are eating, dining, feasting. Instead of thinking about food as something to consume, eating out shows us that food is an experience. You don't have to trade health for pleasure – you can have both.

Here are a few tips for taking the anxiety out of eating out:

- ✪ Remember, it's just one meal.
- ✪ Choose what you fancy and eat with no strings attached – no guilt, no restriction, no 'I'll burn it off tomorrow'.
- ✪ Portion servings can be quite big in some restaurants but that doesn't mean you have to overeat. Eat it all if you want to, but leave some if you don't.
- ✪ Remember that food is just one part of eating out. If it is making you feel anxious, shift your focus to other parts of the experience, such as the people you are with, the conversations you are having and the memories you are making.

FOOD SHOPPING
Moving away from the dieting mentality and realising that food doesn't have to be divided into extremes of 'good' and 'bad' takes the stress and anxiety out of food shopping. Yes, fill your shopping basket with colourful fruits, fresh vegetables and wholefoods that nourish your body, but there is nothing wrong with popping in a box of delicious chocolates or a bottle of your favourite wine to enjoy with friends too.

Here are a few tips to take the anxiety out of food shopping:

- ✪ Go at a time when you are not hungry so you make intuitive, mindful choices over what you are buying instead of letting your old diet mentality creep in.
- ✪ 'Practise the pause' so you don't let unnecessary rules and restrictions interfere with your food choices.
- ✪ Create a list of weekly basics that you can buy without even thinking, such as vegetables, fruit, eggs, yogurt and beans.
- ✪ Buy one new food every week to introduce variety into your diet and make food fun.
- ✪ Find a local farmers' market. Speaking to the people who grow the food you buy will help you experience food in a completely different way.

GROW YOUR OWN
A fun way to build a fear-free relationship with food is to grow your own. You don't have to get an allotment or create a giant vegetable patch – I grow a few herbs on my kitchen windowsill and have a couple of buckets on my balcony with strawberry plants and carrots in. This helps you to further let go of the diet mentality and reduces anxiety around food by shifting your perception of food as a collection of calories and nutrients to a nourishing relationship between sunlight, soil, grower, cook and eater.

Homegrown strawberries!

FEAR-FREE EATING...

...is eating in a way that increases your health and happiness and involves making food choices based on nutrition, pleasure, intuition, tradition and connection.

...is an understanding that we eat for many reasons, including for health, pleasure, tradition, connection with others and connection with nature.

...means shedding the anxiety about getting fat, getting sick and being judged, which causes us to worry about what we eat.

...is the opposite of fear-based eating, where food choices are driven by nutrition myths, diet rules and food anxiety.

...rejects clean eating, calorie counting, vegan or raw food diets, and Paleo and ketogenic diets if they are reducing the quality of your life.

...includes giving up the dieting mentality, trusting your body and giving yourself unconditional permission to eat.

For more tools see: www.FearFreeFood.co.uk

PART 2
FEAR-FREE NUTRITION

Eating nutritious food is important but nutrition doesn't have to be an overriding priority all the time. After all, nutrition is just one element of eating; pleasure, intuition, tradition, practicality and connection are important too. However, *Fear-Free Food* isn't about ignoring nutrition altogether. It's not about eating with complete disregard for the impact food will have on your health, nor is it about obsessing over nutrients. It's about balance: being mindful but not neurotic, aware but not obsessive.

I felt it was important to include a section on nutrition to dispel common nutrition myths that can make us feel anxious or guilty around food and to give you the confidence to make food choices that you know will nourish you.

My hope is that, after reading this section, you have a deeper understanding of how amazing food can make you feel based on the nutrients it contains. This awareness will help as you get to know your body and find a way of eating that works for you.

You will get the most out of this section if you put your current beliefs about nutrition to one side and open your mind to the possibility that the thoughts you currently have may be wrong (because a lot of the information out there is wrong!). Having an open mind will give you the opportunity to discover knowledge that can help you build a fear-free relationship with food.

It is beyond the scope of this book to provide anything other than general advice. If you think you need personalised support from a professional, especially if you are extremely undernourished or have health issues, then please seek it. You can find more information and support at: www.FearFreeFood.co.uk

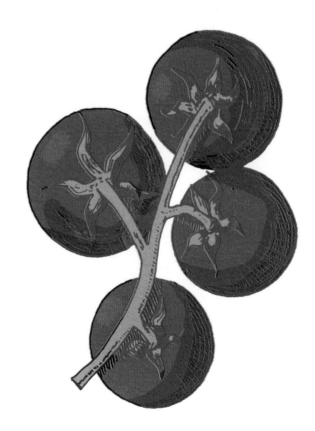

Calories

As calorie counts are printed on the front of most food products these days, it is good to have a basic understanding of what a calorie actually is.

A calorie (kcal) is a unit of energy. In the context of nutrition, calories refer to the energy we consume through food and drink and the energy we expend through physical activity and basic body functions such as breathing, circulation, and digestion. In everyday language, both 1g protein and 1g carbohydrate contain approximately 4kcal; 1g fat contains 9kcal; and 1g alcohol contains 7kcal.

HOW MANY CALORIES SHOULD YOU EAT?

In the UK, the NHS currently recommends that a woman should consume around 2000 calories a day and men should consume 2500 to maintain their weight. American authorities recommend no more than 2200 for women and 2500 for men, while Australian experts recommend 2080 for the average adult and the United Nations recommends the average adult should eat no less than 1800 a day. I'm not sharing these conflicting recommendations to confuse you or to encourage you to count calories, I'm sharing them to highlight how there is no consensus, even among experts, on how many calories we need to consume (so it's not surprising so many of us feel anxious about them!).

In reality, how many calories we need to consume to be healthy is far more complex than these recommendations and depends on lots of factors, including height, weight, age, body composition, genetic predispositions, how much we currently eat and our activity levels.

DO I NEED TO COUNT CALORIES?

The short answer? No. And, in fact, while counting calories isn't inherently harmful, it can increase anxiety and guilt around food and impair quality of life. In a recent study looking at the relationship between calorie-counting apps, fitness trackers and eating disorder symptoms, researchers warned that tracking calories (in terms of calories burned through exercise as well as those consumed in food and drink) can trigger, maintain and exacerbate disordered eating for some people.

I have seen first-hand with clients how calorie counting has got out of control to the point where diet tracking apps have become a compulsion. And I've been there too – there was a time when I felt I had to log everything I ate and if I went over my allotted calories for the day I felt like a failure. I developed a spreadsheet-like relationship with food where, instead of seeing food, I just saw numbers.

If you are trapped in a diet mentality, then tracking calories is only likely to keep you stuck there. It is worth noting that it is not the calorie counting itself that it is the problem but the way it can negatively impact your life. If you already have a fear-free relationship with food, eat largely based on hunger and satisfaction, and calories feel pretty neutral (rather than triggering feelings of guilt and anxiety) then having a general sense of calories can help guide your food choices from time to time – for example, if you have a busy day and you need to eat practically because you may not have opportunity to eat for five or six hours. But, if you end up focusing on calorie consumption and expenditure at the expense of the pleasure and nourishment you get from eating, and the enjoyment and empowerment you can get from exercise, then it is healthier to move to a more intuitive way of eating.

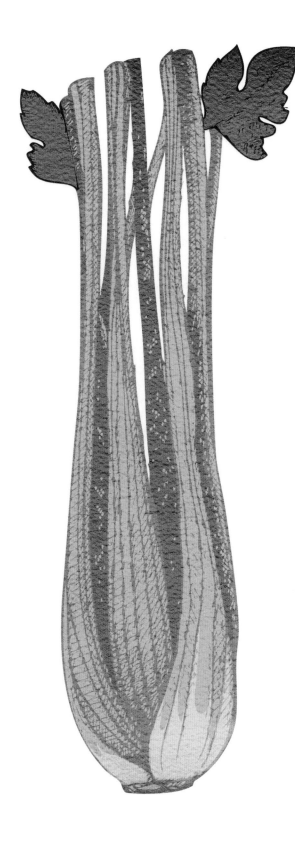

COMMON CALORIE MYTHS

✪ *If calories in equal calories out, then you maintain your weight.*
This is an oversimplification of how both food and your body works. Your body is far more complex than a calculator and while this equation may give you a basic blueprint, it can be deceiving and lead to you under- or overeating as well as over-exercising.

✪ *A calorie is just a calorie.*
One way to move away from obsessive calorie counting is to understand that our body is far more complex than simply transforming all the calories contained in food into energy. The amount of calories we absorb can differ because some foods have more calories available to digestion. For example, when you eat 150 calories' worth of nuts, you may absorb a different amount of calories to when you eat 150 calories of banana. This is related to how much fibre a food contains, digestive enzyme activity from eating different foods and the thermic effect it has (how many calories are required to digest it).

✪ *Everybody processes calories in the same way.*
In fact, as well as absorbing different amounts of calories depending on what type of food you eat, you and your friend might absorb a different amount of calories even if you eat the same food. This is related to our gut microbes, intestine length and the presence of certain digestive enzymes.

✪ *To lose one pound of weight (about 0.5kg) you need to create a 3500 calorie deficit.*
It's been estimated that this figure appears on over 35,000 weight-loss sites so it's not surprising that many people accept this as truth. However, it's a gross oversimplification of how your body works and ignores metabolic adaptations, gender and changes in eating and exercise habits. Using the 3500-calorie-per-pound rule is not accurate and can set you up for disappointment so counting calories in this way is just not worth doing.

Nutrients

Nutrients are molecules found in food that provide nourishment for life and growth. They can be divided into two main categories: macronutrients and micronutrients. These days a lot of us think about food only in terms of nutrients. For instance, there was a time when I focused on eating 'more protein'. It got to the point where, instead of seeing food as a source of nourishment (let alone pleasure and connection with others), I just saw it in terms of how many grams of protein, fat and carbs it contained.

In order to develop a fear-free relationship with food, it's helpful to talk about food as *food*. So, if you want to increase your protein intake, think about 'eating more protein-rich foods' rather than 'eating more protein' – it's a subtle difference, but it can have a huge impact on reconnecting you to food as more than simply the sum of its chemical parts.

MACRONUTRIENTS

Macronutrients are nutrients that are needed in large amounts ('macro' means large). These are: carbohydrates, fats and proteins.

CARBOHYDRATES

Carbohydrates are converted by your body to be used for energy. They can be simple (a single sugar molecule) or complex (multiple sugar molecules) and both can be healthy food options. Foods that are high in simple carbohydrates include fruit, dairy products and anything where sugar is added, such as cakes and biscuits. Foods high in complex carbohydrates (starches) include wholegrains, potatoes, green vegetables and beans. Government and research-based recommendations for carbohydrate intake vary from 45 to 65 per cent of your diet (around half of each meal), but you may feel better eating slightly more or slightly less. You'll probably find you feel more energised after eating foods that are high in carbohydrates that contain other nutrients and fibre (these tend to be wholefoods, such as fruit and vegetables), than you do after eating foods high in simple carbohydrates with little nutritional value (these tend to be high-sugar, processed foods).

To put it simply, you'll likely feel much better eating foods containing carbohydrates in their natural form, such as fruit, vegetables and wholegrains, most of the time, and keeping foods higher in simple sugars and low in other nutrients, such as cake, for when you really fancy them. Personally, I love a slice of carrot cake with my coffee but I'm pretty sure if I ate it for every meal I would end up feeling sluggish and slightly nauseous (and that's not how I want to feel!), whereas I eat carrots almost daily (boiled, roasted or grated into a stir-fry) as they leave me feeling nourished and energised.

FATS

Fats are made up of chains of molecules which store lots of energy in the chemical bonds. This means they are a high-density source of energy. Some fatty acids are essential to help us absorb certain vitamins and balance our hormones. Dietary fats can be divided into:

- ✪ Saturated fats (found in foods such as red meat, full-fat dairy products and coconut oil).
- ✪ Monounsaturated fats (found in foods such as nuts, avocados and olive oil).
- ✪ Polyunsaturated fats (found in foods such as oily fish such as salmon and mackerel).
- ✪ Trans fats (found in foods such as margarine and some cakes and biscuits).

It is widely accepted now that trans fats are not good for your health, but there is still controversy among nutrition scientists over how much saturated and unsaturated fat is optimal. As a guide, I would recommend getting anywhere from 20 to 35 per cent of energy from fat. If you look at traditional diets, this happens quite naturally. For example, Sardinians (a population with one of the highest rates of longevity and lowest rates of chronic disease) are known for their consumption of sardines (rich in polyunsaturated fats), olive oil (high in monounsaturated fats) and goat's cheese (rich in saturated fat).

PROTEINS

Proteins are compounds made up of chains of amino acids. Eating foods containing protein is essential for cell growth and repair, and to regulate body functions such as enzyme activity and metabolism. Proteins containing all nine essential amino acids (those the body cannot produce itself) are found in animal products such as meat and dairy. Vegetables, legumes (beans and lentils) and rice also contain protein but not all essential amino acids when eaten in isolation – these are often referred to as 'incomplete proteins'. This it isn't something that you need to worry about as, when you're eating without restriction, you'll find you get the full range of amino acids over the course of a few days and will naturally eat foods in combinations that create complete proteins. For example, lentil curry is traditionally served with rice in Sri Lanka, hummus is served with pitta bread in the Middle East, and we in the UK eat peanut butter with wholegrain bread – all these meals contain complete proteins. Again, protein recommendations vary considerably among experts but it is generally advised that anywhere between 10 and 35 per cent of your diet should be made up of high-protein foods.

I know the recommendations I have given here aren't precise, but that's because, as humans, we do pretty well eating most things. You don't need to eat every macronutrient at every meal, or even every day – remember that balance is achieved over a period of time. Simply make sure that over the course of a few days you're getting a good variety of protein-rich, fat-rich and carb-rich foods, and don't deliberately exclude any of them.

COMMON MACRONUTRIENT MYTHS

✪ *Carbs are fattening.*
Low-carb diets are incredibly common for fear-based eaters because of concerns that carbohydrates are fattening. In reality, research suggests that the ratio of carbohydrates in your diet compared to fat doesn't have any significant effect on your weight. A diet slightly higher in protein (around 20 per cent) can help with weight management for some people, but this still means that, regardless of your health and fitness goals, you can choose foods according to taste, practicality and personal preferences rather than the amount of carbs they contain.

✪ *Fats are unhealthy.*
Lipophobia (the fear of dietary fat) is just as common as anxiety around carbs. Many of us believe that eating fat will make us fat. Like too much of anything, eating too much fat will make you gain weight, but fat itself is not the problem. Our anxiety around fat can be traced back to the way nutrition advice on fats has changed over the years. For example, saturated fats used to be thought of as the cause of heart disease so the advice was to replace butter with margarine. Now research has shown that the trans fats in margarine are dangerous and saturated fat isn't so bad after all. The same is true for avocados – once they were viewed as a high-fat food to be avoided, but now they're treated as a 'superfood' because they are rich in monounsaturated fat which has been associated with reduced risk of heart disease. It can be pretty confusing! But this confusion doesn't mean dietary fat is something we need to fear and it is worth exploring how eating more high-fat foods affects your energy, digestion, skin and memory. This doesn't mean we need to take things to the extreme and consume fat in huge amounts like many ketogenic or low-carb, high-fat diets are suggesting – nutrition science is still too young to make any definite recommendations on extreme diets such as these.

✪ *Protein is the most important macronutrient.* There is no doubt that protein is important, but there is no need to prioritise it in all meals (especially if it's at the expense of eating a greater variety of foods). Of course there are times, such as after exercise, when increasing the amount of protein you eat through protein-rich foods or supplements will help your body to recover from your workout, but the main concern is that if you focus on eating foods high in protein, you could be missing out on other essential nutrients. From personal experience, I found that when I was overconsuming foods high in protein, I was consequently undereating other nutrients which left me feeling exhausted.

MICRONUTRIENTS

Like macronutrients, micronutrients are molecules our bodies need to make energy, only in much smaller amounts. Micronutrients play an important role in the prevention and treatment of certain diseases as well as in bone health and metabolism regulation. They can be divided into two types: vitamins and minerals.

Foods that contain a high amount of vitamins and minerals in proportion to their calories are often termed 'nutrient dense'. These foods include: almonds, berries, broccoli, Brussels sprouts, cauliflower, kale, lentils and sunflower seeds. I find that by eating a selection of these nutrient-dense foods most days, I have good energy, I can focus on my work, I sleep well and my yoga practice is strong.

VITAMINS

Vitamins are either water-soluble or fat-soluble. Water-soluble vitamins are lost through bodily fluids so need to be replaced daily (for example, vitamin C, which can be found in foods including peppers, leafy greens, berries and citrus fruits, and the B-complex vitamins, which can be found in a diverse range of foods from eggs and organ meats to tofu and legumes depending on the type of B vitamin). Fat-soluble vitamins tend to be stored in the body so aren't needed daily. For example, high levels of vitamin A are found in liver, egg yolks and butter from grass-fed cows; oily fish is high in vitamin D; and kale, Brussels sprouts and cabbage provide a good source of vitamin K.

MINERALS

Unlike vitamins, which are organic and come from plants or animals, generally speaking, minerals are inorganic chemical elements that we usually consume in salt form. They are essential for bone health, hormone production, brain function and supporting healthy muscles. Macrominerals (those we need larger amounts of) include calcium, magnesium and sodium, while trace minerals (those we need smaller amounts of) include iron, zinc and selenium.

Just as with macronutrients, you don't need to obsess over getting every micronutrient at each meal. The best way to get the vitamins and minerals your body needs is to eat as large a variety of foods as possible, including 7–10 portions of fruit and vegetables a day, and limit restriction of any food groups unless you have a diagnosed allergy or health issue that could be made worse by eating certain foods.

It would take the rest of the book to go into detail about nutrients, their functions and where to get them from, so I've included more information at: www.FearFreeFood.co.uk

Supplements

A dietary supplement is any edible product that contains ingredients intended to add further nutritional value to your diet. This includes vitamin pills, protein powders and herbal supplements.

Fear-based beliefs around supplements tend to be based on one of two extremes:

1. Wholefoods are always superior to supplements because supplements are 'synthetic'.
2. Supplements are superior to wholefoods because we can't get all the nutrients we need from food.

However, nutrition is just not this black and white. Most people can get all the nutrients they need from foods if they are eating in a balanced way, but there are certainly times when supplements can be helpful, and even necessary. I know I found supplementing my diet with protein shakes incredibly beneficial when I was a competitive weightlifter because it helped me recover from my training and stopped me worrying about eating enough protein-rich foods at mealtimes (this worked for me, but it might not work for you!).

COMMON SUPPLEMENT MYTHS:

✪ *More is better.*
A lot of people will take a 'just in case' approach to supplements – they'll supplement their diet with extra nutrients in the form of vitamins, minerals and protein powders, 'just in case' they aren't getting them from their food. However, just because a little bit of something is good for you, doesn't mean a lot of it is even better. We don't have enough scientific evidence about the long-term safety of high doses of supplements to recommend this generic approach. So, like everything when it comes to nutrition, it's about getting enough nutrients, but not too much. There is no cookie-cutter approach, so if you are experiencing health issues you feel could be related to nutrient deficiencies then it is worth getting blood tests done to explore whether it would be helpful for you to take certain supplements.

✪ *You need to take supplements all year round.*
In the same way that eating seasonally helps us get a large variety of vitamins in our diet from the fruits and vegetables that are in season, adjusting which supplements we take depending on the season can also help prevent deficiencies and ensure we don't take high doses of supplements unnecessarily. For example, Public Health England recommends we supplement our diet with 10mcg vitamin D (needed for healthy bones, teeth and muscle) during autumn and winter. Vitamin D is found in a small number of foods but the main source is via sunlight on our skin and, because the sun in the UK isn't strong enough for us to produce vitamin D during the winter months and it's difficult for us to get enough from food alone, supplementing can prevent deficiencies. However, during the spring and summer months most of us can get enough vitamin D from sunlight so supplementing with vitamin D may not be required.

Common Food Fears

The rise of 'clean eating' has led to certain foods and food groups becoming demonised. The vilification of specific foods probably wasn't the intention of those behind the clean eating movement, but is rather an unhealthy consequence of the extremism of our diet culture. For example, many of my clients who come to me with a fear-based relationship with food interpret advice that 'If eaten in excess, gluten can irritate the intestinal villi in the gut' as 'I should never eat gluten ever again'. Remember, moderation doesn't mean elimination.

From gluten and sugar to meat and soya, there will always be some expert somewhere who blacklists a certain food. I hope the information below eases your anxiety around foods that are commonly demonised by the diet industry and tend to cause the most confusion.

GLUTEN

While some clean eating blogs have called it 'the devil', gluten is absolutely not that. It's nothing more than a family of proteins found in grains such as wheat, rye, spelt and barley. It's estimated that up to a third of us are trying to cut out gluten from our diet, yet most of us don't really know why. While coeliac disease (an allergy to gluten) is a serious condition (and if you think you may have it then you should ask your doctor to be tested), it only affects around 1 per cent of the population in Europe and the USA, and there is still debate among professionals as to what extent non-coeliac gluten sensitivity exists.

Like me in the past, you may have cut out gluten from your diet and felt better for doing so. However, this may not be directly because of the exclusion of gluten. It could be because of the 'placebo effect' – whereby you believe you feel better without any real therapeutic benefits. (There is also a 'nocebo effect' with gluten – when people following a gluten-free diet are told they have consumed gluten when in reality they haven't, they still report 'symptoms' related to gluten intake.) You may also feel less

sluggish, for instance. because, by cutting out gluten, you have started eating more fruit, vegetables and nutritious foods that your body thrives on.

You never have to eat gluten again, but if avoiding gluten is having a negative impact on your life then it is worth considering adding it back into your diet. When I was unnecessarily following a gluten-free diet, food shopping and eating was a stressful experience. One of the things that inspired me to reintroduce gluten to my diet was seeing a photo of myself when I was about five tucking into a large slice of a French baguette and it reminded me that, as a kid, I used to eat gluten regularly, without any adverse effects. If, like me, you were able to eat gluten without any symptoms when you were younger but have now jumped on the gluten-free diet bandwagon, then it might be worth experimenting with how you feel reintroducing it so you can eat with more freedom.

If you feel particularly anxious about wheat, then start off by experimenting with other grains such as rye and spelt (try baking my Seedy Soda Bread, page 182). Eating sourdough bread is also a good option as it's easier to digest because of the fermentation of the dough. And there is something very nourishing about going to a local bakery instead of a supermarket to get a loaf of their properly fermented, freshly baked bread. Of course there are more nutritious foods than bread, but sometimes grabbing a sandwich on the go is practical – and doing so every now and then isn't going to do you any harm. Saying that, if you know you experience symptoms from eating gluten and are happier avoiding it then there is nothing wrong with that either – just be sure you are making the choice out of self-love (because you know your choice will make you happier and healthier) and not out of anxiety, deprivation or guilt.

SUGAR

'Sugar is toxic' is a statement that's become increasingly common in healthy eating books and blogs over the last couple of years. Like anything, eat enough of it and it's toxic. But that doesn't mean we need to take things to the extreme and eliminate it from our diet completely. I have clients who took the sugar-as-poison hype to such an extreme they stopped eating fruit because of the fear of fructose (and I've been there too!). Yes, fruit contains sugar but it is also packed full of vitamins, minerals, fibre and antioxidants, making it one of Mother Nature's most nutritious and delicious creations.

Common sense teaches us that eating natural sugars in fruit is more nutritious than eating a biscuit, but fear-free eating is about more than just nutrients. It's about bringing balance into your life, which means eating in a way that adds to the overall quality of your life. This doesn't mean bingeing on sugar-filled foods every day; it means relaxing any extreme anxieties around sugar so that you can have a biscuit or a couple of squares of chocolate when you fancy them without it causing guilt.

The other common scaremongering statement is: 'sugar is addictive'. It's true that we have an innate desire for sweet things because, evolutionarily, sweetness is a sign that the food is full of energy and nutrients (for example, fruit and, from the very beginning of life, breast milk). However, just because we are attracted to sugar-containing foods does not mean we are 'addicted' to them. Of course, the fact that there are now many easy-to-access foods with added sugar which don't contain nutrients (such as baked goods) can confuse our natural instincts, but this doesn't mean that we need to avoid them altogether. In fact, research suggests that any addiction-like behaviours, such as sugar cravings and overeating sugary foods, only occur when sugar is limited. From my experience, my cravings for sugary foods reduced drastically when I stopped treating them as a 'forbidden food' and realised I could eat fruit and the occasional slice of cheesecake without it having any negative effect on my health. If you allow yourself to eat sugar whenever you want, you'll find that it doesn't take that much to satisfy you – even kids get sick of eating sweets eventually!

MEAT AND DAIRY

Cutting out meat and dairy has become increasingly popular over the last decade. According to the Vegan Society, the number of people in the UK going vegan increased by over 350 per cent between 2006 and 2016.

Many people cut out animal products for environmental and ethical reasons (and it is true that a diet high in meat and dairy may not be efficient for feeding a global population), but many health claims over the dangers of eating animal products have been exaggerated by the media, leading to unnecessary fear and confusion.

As far as we know, no population on earth has ever been vegan, and most traditional diets, while being based around plants, include meat and dairy to some extent (for example, Sardinians, one of the healthiest nations on the planet, regularly drink goat's milk and eat meat on average five times a month).

A body of research suggests that, for people who are mindful of their health, there is no difference in lifespan or rates of chronic diseases between vegetarians and omnivores (people who eat both meat and plants). Of course, this doesn't mean we should eat tonnes of meat like some diets, such as the Paleo diet, tend to encourage (and processed meats such as ham and bacon should be eaten sparingly because they have been scientifically linked with cancer), but it does mean that if we feel more energised and grounded when we include a bit of meat and dairy in our diet, we can do so without fear.

BEANS, LEGUMES AND SOYA

The demonisation of beans began when the Paleo diet became popular and we were warned that the phytic acid in beans prevents nutrient absorption. This is a grossly exaggerated statement. Although the phytic acid in beans *does* impair the absorption of some nutrients, like iron and zinc, it is *only for that meal*, and cooking them reduces the phytic acid in them in any case. Beans are so nutritious anyway that it doesn't really matter if some of the nutrients they contain aren't absorbed.

Soya beans in particular seem to cause confusion. Many of my clients have been caught out believing the myth that soya can have a negative effect on your hormones (and can apparently make men grow boobs!). In reality, there is no solid science that soya lowers testosterone, and early research suggests soya may be protective against breast cancer, prostate cancer and osteoporosis. This doesn't mean all soya products are equal though; if you focus on eating soya either in its wholefood form (as soya beans) or as tofu or tempeh, then you'll likely feel better than if you eat it in 'mock meat' burgers, which are generally less nutrient-rich and use filler ingredients.

After avoiding beans for years out of fear they'd suck all the nutrients out of my food, I now eat them in some form every day because I love the diversity of what you can make with them, they help my digestion and they leave me feeling energised.

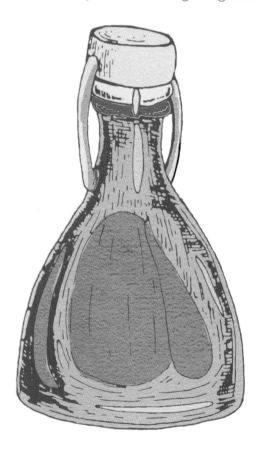

PROCESSED FOODS

The term 'processed food' seems to have become synonymous with 'junk food', and the fear of anything processed is something that the clean-eating trend has unconsciously fostered, making us feel guilty for eating anything that is not in its wholefood form. Of course, it's good to include lots of wholefoods in our diet because they are nutritious, filling and delicious, but that doesn't mean we need to live off raw vegetables alone (cooking is a form of processing). In fact, some methods of processing produce incredibly nutritious foods: yogurt is created through the process of fermentation; we can preserve the nutrients in vegetables through the process of freezing and canning; and nutrient-rich foods such as nut butter, dried fruit, sauerkraut, dark chocolate, tempeh and tomato sauce have all been through some kind of processing.

Letting go of the black-and-white mentality where I saw all wholefoods as good and all processed foods as bad was incredibly healing for my relationship with food. Not only did I used to believe 'processed' meant unhealthy, I thought if I wasn't always baking my own bread from scratch and soaking my own beans, it made me lazy. Understanding that eating processed food doesn't make me unhealthy or lazy has made life so much more practical too – just to be able to buy shop-bought hummus when I don't have time to make my own or grab a falafel wrap for lunch when I'm out for the day allows me to channel my energies into more purposeful directions.

Of course we want to eat the foods that nature intended, but we don't need to deny ourselves modern food. We are living in a constantly evolving world and it's impossible to eat in the same way as our ancestors. It's easy for experts to tell us to avoid all processed foods but there are some great processed and packaged foods that just make it easier and simpler for us to eat well.

Superfoods

'Superfood' has become a buzzword over the last couple of years. While there is no scientific definition, it's widely accepted that a superfood is a nutrient-rich food that some people believe is especially beneficial to health. Popular superfoods include avocados, bee pollen, cacao nibs, chia seeds, flaxseeds, goji berries, kale, maca powder, moringa, and wheatgrass. While these foods are certainly nutritious, there are often huge marketing budgets behind their rise to superfood status and their health benefits have often been overhyped by the media, resulting in food fads. The danger with this is that we end up obsessing over eating a handful of foods that claim to be 'super' while restricting other nutritious and delicious foods because they haven't been given the same health status.

When I was consumed by eating 'clean', I remember making morning 'superfood' smoothies of kale, avocado, chia seeds, flaxseeds and wheatgrass because, even though I would have preferred a bowl of porridge or some scrambled eggs on toast, I thought starting my day with a superfood smoothie was the 'right' thing to do. It tasted disgusting and taught me that health meant depriving myself of the foods I liked and forcing myself to eat the ones I didn't. Now, I happily have my porridge, maybe with a sprinkle of goji berries and raisins for extra sweetness and a spoonful of cacao nibs and chopped nuts for added crunch.

Nutrition science is complex, and it is far too simple to class some foods as 'super' and not others. We can't look at individual foods outside the context of the rest of our diet. And the truth is, if you're not nourishing your body with nutritious foods most of the time, adding in a couple of superfoods is not going to make much difference. Equally, if you are eating a balanced diet, full of fruits and vegetables, do regular exercise and make time for connection and relaxation, eating a couple of superfoods won't make much difference either.

Healthy Eating

I have purposely limited my use of the term 'healthy eating' throughout the book because it has become synonymous with 'dieting' and there is no real consensus on what healthy eating actually means.

Nutritionally, there is still a lot about food we do not know. Because of this, any diet or 'healthy eating lifestyle' that promotes rigid rules and restrictions is likely to be based on myths and exaggerated health claims. I have been sucked into pretty much all these healthy eating regimes and I promise you they will not make you any healthier or happier. In fact, they will only foster anxiety around food and guilt around eating.

What you can do, from looking at the nutrition science discussed in this section as well as the traditional diets of our ancestors, is adopt a guiding nutrition principle that will give you the confidence to make food choices that support both your health and happiness.

This principle echoes the words of food journalist, Michael Pollan:

'Eat food. Not too much. Mostly plants.'

When it comes to fear-free eating, I would amend this guiding principle slightly:

'Eat food. Not too much. Not too little. Mostly plants.'

To explain this further, most of the time we want to base our food choices around minimally processed, plant-based foods because these are the foods that will nourish us and leave us feeling energised.

'Most of the time' is an incredibly important part of this principle, and I would say it translates into about 80 per cent of your food choices being based around wholefoods you enjoy. The other 20 per cent of food choices may focus less on eating for nutrition and health and more on pleasure and connection. I found that when I let go of rigid rules and began fear-free eating, this 80/20 principle happened quite naturally. I intuitively wanted wholefoods like lentil curries, vegetable stir-fries and fresh fruit salads *most of the time*, but every now and then I got a hankering for something like a freshly baked scone with clotted cream. Although it might not have been as nutritious scientifically, it nourished me in other ways. For me, this is healthy eating.

As adults, we get to take responsibility for what healthy eating means for us based on what makes us feel good. It's great to learn about nutrition, and having a basic understanding of the nutrients foods contain can be helpful in guiding food choices (for example, you might choose a wholegrain bread over white bread because it is higher in fibre if you know that eating a high-fibre diet helps with your digestion). But, in order to let go of a dieting mentality, many of my clients find it helpful to deemphasise nutrition science and focus on other elements of eating, such as how different foods make them feel in terms of energy and satiety and how much pleasure and satisfaction they get from eating them.

Your ideas about healthy eating will continually evolve so it's not something you need to stress over setting in stone right now. In fact, stressing over healthy eating can do more harm than good. I found that when I relaxed around healthy eating, my stress levels went down, I slept better and I had more time and energy to dedicate to the things that gave my life meaning – and all those things will be far more beneficial to your health than achieving nutritional perfection.

FEAR-FREE NUTRITION...

...acknowledges that nutrition is highly personalised so following a generic diet plan from a book or blog will probably not help you in becoming healthier or happier.

...should feel neutral without any judgement, anxiety or guilt attached to calories, nutrients or specific foods.

...recognises that, although not all foods are nutritionally equal, if you're eating a balanced diet without restricting any food groups, then you'll likely be getting all the nutrients you need.

...dispels the many myths around gluten, sugar, meat and processed foods that have caused unnecessary anxiety and confusion, which in reality can all be included in your diet as long as you have no allergies or intolerances.

...recommends basing your food choices around minimally processed, plant-based foods most of the time to nourish your body and leave you feeling energised.

...is about ditching the idea of the 'perfect diet' and using your time and energy doing things that will reduce your stress, help you relax and nourish your soul. Instead of wasting time analysing nutrition labels or getting confused over exaggerated health claims, spend more time in nature, enjoy socialising with friends, start meditating or get to bed earlier.

PART 3
FEAR-FREE RECIPES

I never really learned how to cook when I was younger. I was born in the nineties and pretty much lived off Marmite sandwiches, turkey dinosaurs and potato smiles as a kid. This was partly because I was a fussy eater and partly because my mum worked full-time and chucking some frozen potato waffles in the oven was about all she had the energy for at the end of a long day (she never learned to cook either so didn't realise how quick and easy cooking meals from scratch could be). So, if, like me, you never quite got the hang of preparing good-quality food for yourself at home, this section is all about upping your kitchen game, helping you understand flavours, showing you how to make both nutritious and delicious meals, inspiring you to try new dishes and getting you excited about food again.

I didn't learn how to cook properly until a few years ago. I'd started doing all the other adult stuff – changing lightbulbs, taking electricity readings, submitting my tax return ... but I'd still never learned to cook. Sure, I could chuck a load of vegetables in a pan and call it a stir-fry and boil a couple of eggs without too much trouble, but my fear-based relationship with food had meant that the less adventurous I was in the kitchen, the easier it was to control what I was eating. As my relationship with food improved, I found that sourcing ingredients, preparing food and cooking meals helped me to reconnect with the enjoyment of eating. I started to experiment with recipes at home, got cooking lessons when I travelled to different countries, hosted dinner parties and slowly taught myself how to cook. Okay, so I burned some stuff and made a heck of a lot of mess along the way, but after plenty of practice, I have created my 'Fear-Free

Recipes' section to save you time, mess, dry cakes and burnt cookies, and to show you the basics so you can create delicious and healthy meals.

I've developed these recipes with five things in mind: pleasure, nutrition, practicality, connection and tradition. I have been inspired by traditional meals eaten by people in the Blue Zones (see page 22), and spoken to friends from all over the world to learn about their favourite family meals, all the time being mindful of nutrition science to ensure the recipes help you get all the nutrients your body needs. I have created recipes that avoid common complaints (the main ones seem to be: 'faddy', 'overpriced ingredients', 'time-consuming', 'pretentious and patronising', 'not realistic for working people', 'unoriginal and unexciting').

So, the recipes you will find in this book aren't faddy or time-consuming, you can get all the ingredients fairly cheaply in your local supermarket and they are family-friendly. They are inspired by lots of cultures, flavours and ingredients, and there are lots of different options depending on how much time you have, who you're cooking for and what kind of food you fancy.

You'll also find that most of the recipes are based around plants (fruit, vegetables or legumes) because most people find that these are the foods that make them feel healthiest and happiest. The recipes also reflect the guiding nutrition principle of *Fear-Free Food*: 'Eat food. Not too much. Not too little. Mostly plants' (see page 68). The inclusion of lots of plants isn't just for their health benefits – they add to the flavour, texture and enjoyment of each dish. For example, the Japanese have been putting beans in their cakes for centuries so you'll find a Chocolate Berry Bean Cake on page 192. You'll find recipes for Roasted Courgette Coins (page 176), Spicy Sweet Potato Wedges (page 168), Lemon and Almond Green Beans (page 176) and lots of other ways to jazz up your plants in the Sides, Sauces, Dips and Dressings section (pages 167–179). Of course, if you feel better when you eat meat then feel free to add a meat-based side dish to your meal such as the Honey and Sesame Steak Strips (page 170).

The recipes in this book are designed to inspire you, not restrain you. You know what you like so trust yourself, taste as you go and make the recipes your own. The options are endless – just use your intuition and think about what role the ingredient plays in the recipe (for example, seasoning, texture, protein source, etc.).

When it comes to quantities, you'll find I sometimes refer to grams and sometimes to teaspoons or tablespoons depending on what I think will be easiest for you. For example, in the recipes for Busy Weekday Breakfasts (pages 77–89) I often refer to spoon measurements because you probably don't have time to weigh out everything. But in recipes where you need to be a bit more accurate with your ingredients, I give a specific amount in grams.

Cooking isn't rocket science – have fun with it! And if you want more recipes head to: www.FearFreeFood.co.uk.

Kitchen Essentials

EQUIPMENT

Having the right kitchen tools makes cooking a whole lot easier. You don't need anything fancy like a spiraliser or expensive blender, but it's helpful to get these basics to begin with:

- Airtight containers
- Baking dish
- Baking trays
- Chef's knife
- Chopping boards
- Colander
- Cooling rack
- Digital scales
- Fish slice/turner
- Grater
- Hand/stick blender
- Measuring jug
- Measuring spoons
- Microwave
- Mini food processor
- Mixing bowls
- Non-stick frying pan
- Peeler
- Small and large saucepans
- Serrated knife
- Spatula
- Steamer
- Tin opener
- Wok
- Wooden spoons

INGREDIENTS

Most of the recipes that follow contain fresh ingredients that you'll want to restock once or twice a week, but it's good to have a selection of store cupboard staples so you'll never be far from a simple, healthy meal. This might look like a long list of ingredients so build it up over time as you explore new recipes.

Store cupboard

- your favourite grains: couscous, oats, quinoa, rice (including microwave rice)
- your favourite pasta: farfalle, shells, rice noodles
- your favourite wraps or tortillas: corn, wholegrain
- your favourite tinned beans: chickpeas, cannellini beans, kidney beans, mixed beans, lentils
- your favourite nuts and seeds: almonds, cashews, walnuts, sesame seeds, sunflower seeds
- a couple of nut butters: almond, cashew, peanut, tahini
- baking basics: almond extract, baking powder, bicarbonate of soda, chocolate chips, cocoa powder, desiccated coconut, dried apricots, raisins, vanilla extract, 85 per cent cocoa dark chocolate
- a couple of flours: coconut, plain, spelt, wholegrain
- your favourite sweeteners: brown sugar, caster sugar, runny honey, maple syrup
- your favourite tinned fish: salmon, sardines, tuna
- your favourite oils: coconut oil, olive oil, toasted sesame oil
- your favourite vinegar: apple cider vinegar, rice vinegar, white wine vinegar
- your favourite spices: black pepper, chilli, cinnamon, coriander, cumin, smoked paprika, turmeric
- a couple of condiments and flavourings: soy sauce, stock cubes, sun-dried tomatoes, pesto, pickled beetroot, wholegrain mustard
- tinned tomatoes
- sea salt

Fresh stuff

- aromatics: ginger, garlic, onion
- lemon or lime
- free range eggs (unless otherwise stated, all eggs in the recipes that follow are medium)
- your favourite milk: almond, cashew, coconut, cow's, goat's, soya (feel free to choose whatever milk you like best)
- your favourite yogurt: coconut, Greek, natural, soya
- a couple of protein-rich foods: beef strips, cod, chicken breasts, prawns, salmon, tofu
- a couple of cheeses: feta, halloumi, mozzarella
- your favourite vegetables: aubergine, broccoli, butternut squash, carrots, cauliflower, courgette, green beans, kale, tomatoes, peppers
- your favourite fruits: apples, bananas, mangoes, pineapples, pears

Freezer basics

- your favourite frozen vegetables: cauliflower, green beans, peas, spinach, sweetcorn
- your favourite frozen berries: blackberries, blueberries, raspberries

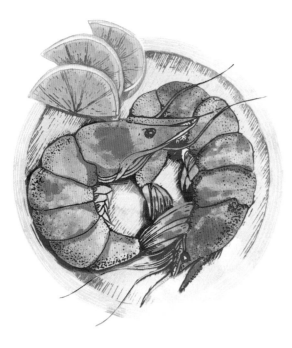

HOW TO...

COOK, STORE AND REHEAT RICE
Cooking

White and basmati rice: Place 50–75g rice per person into a sieve and rinse under cold water to remove excess starch (this will stop the grains from sticking together when cooked). Bring a large pan of water to the boil with a pinch of salt and add the rice. Stir once and, once the grains of rice have started dancing around, cover and simmer for 10 minutes, or until the rice is tender. Drain through a sieve, rinse with boiling water and serve. If you have time, for a softer, fluffier rice, pre-soak the rice in cold water for 20–30 minutes before cooking.

Brown rice: Follow the above instructions but simmer the rice for 25–30 minutes, or until the rice is soft.

Storing

If you are batch cooking rice or have some leftover that you want to use the next day, it is important to cool the rice as quickly as you can (ideally within an hour). Either divide the rice into smaller servings once cooked and leave to cool or place the rice in a colander and run under cold water for a couple of minutes. Once cooled, store it in an airtight container or resealable plastic bag in the fridge for up to three days or in the freezer for up to one month. You should only reheat rice once, so it's a good idea to portion it out before freezing to avoid any waste.

Reheating

If you are reheating rice from the fridge, simply empty it into a microwaveable bowl with one or two tablespoons of water. Cover and heat on medium high for 2–3 minutes until steaming hot all the way through (you might want to experiment with your microwave to see how long it takes). Alternatively, you can empty the rice into a pan with one to two tablespoons of water and stir-fry until heated through.

Use the same methods to reheat frozen rice, just allow a little longer cooking time for the rice to defrost and heat through.

HOW TO...

PREPARE TOFU FOR COOKING
Tofu is a brilliantly versatile ingredient that is packed full of protein and soaks up flavours like a sponge, but it has a reputation for being slimy, which can put people off. Choose a firm or extra-firm tofu (rather than silken) and select the method below depending on how much time you have.

For when you want to cook with it immediately
Simply drain the water off the tofu, wrap it in a couple of sheets of kitchen roll and squeeze it gently to remove any excess water.

For when you're preparing it in advance
Preparing tofu a couple of hours before cooking will give you a slightly firmer texture. Simply follow the above instructions and then leave the wrapped tofu in a dish weighted with a couple of heavy objects on top to squeeze out more water (I usually place a baking tray on top and load it up with books!). Leave it in the fridge for at least 30 minutes or ideally overnight before unwrapping and using in your recipe.

HOW TO...

COOK SKINLESS CHICKEN BREASTS
Skinless chicken breasts can sometimes be dry and chewy when cooked incorrectly. Follow the simple guidelines below to ensure your chicken is always moist and tender.

In a pan
Flatten the chicken breasts using the bottom of a glass jar or a meat hammer until they are 2–3cm thick. Season with a little salt and pepper. Heat a large frying pan (that you've got a lid for) until hot and add one tablespoon of olive oil. Swirl to coat the pan evenly. Turn the heat down to medium and add the chicken breasts. Cook for 1 minute until the breasts start to go a little golden, before flipping them over, turning the heat down to low and placing the lid on the pan. Leave for 10 minutes without taking the lid off and then turn off the heat. Leave the lid on the pan for another 10 minutes as the chicken breasts will continue to poach in their own juices. Check the chicken is cooked all the way through (with no pink in the middle), slice, serve or leave to cool and store in an airtight container in the fridge for up to four days.

In the oven
Preheat the oven to 200°C. Flatten the chicken breasts, as above, brush both sides with olive oil and place on a baking tray. Season with a little salt and pepper or use any herbs or spices you like for extra flavour. Bake in the oven for 15–20 minutes depending on the size of your chicken breasts. Check each breast is cooked all the way through with no pink in the middle and leave to rest in the juices for about 5 minutes to make the chicken extra succulent. Slice, shred, dice or serve whole.

Busy Weekday Breakfasts

Weekday mornings can be a little hectic so these breakfast ideas are perfect for when you're short on time.

Strawberry Cheesecake Thickie

This breakfast is like a smoothie but thicker and creamier! It is great for when you're in a rush but need something energising to fuel you up for the morning. Strawberries are my favourite fruit, but you can experiment with whatever you like best – mangoes and pineapples make a lovely tropical thickie, and blueberries and raspberries add a delicious summery zing.

Serves 1

- 100g frozen strawberries
- 40g oats
- 30g low-fat cream cheese or silken tofu
- 150ml milk
- 0–1 tbsp honey, to taste
- 3 ice cubes

Place all the ingredients in a blender and blend for 2–3 minutes until the mixture is thick and creamy.

Tropical Overnight Oats

Nothing says summer quite like coconut, mango and pineapple. These overnight oats are perfect for mornings when you want to start your day with something fresh and fruity. They give you a great balance of macronutrients to keep you energised and you can prepare them in less than five minutes the night before and just grab them from the fridge in the morning.

Serves 2

- 90g oats
- 80ml tinned coconut milk
- 80ml milk
- 100g Greek yogurt (or dairy-free alternative)
- 1 tbsp chia seeds or flaxseeds (optional – adds thickness)
- 1–2 tsp honey or maple syrup, to taste
- 1 banana, mashed
- 50g mango, fresh or defrosted from frozen, diced
- 50g pineapple, fresh or tinned, diced
- 2 tbsp toasted coconut flakes

Place all the ingredients except the coconut flakes in a large bowl and stir to combine. Divide between two jars or bowls and leave in the fridge for at least four hours or overnight.

In the morning, top your oats with the coconut flakes or some extra chopped fruit before serving.

Apple Crumble Yogurt Bowl

This yogurt bowl is the perfect breakfast for when you need a little midweek pick-me-up. The Greek yogurt is creamy and full of protein; the granola is crunchy and provides a good source of carbs; the walnuts are beautifully buttery and are full of healthy fats; and the caramelised apples elevate a simple, nutritious breakfast into something a little more luxurious. Caramelised pineapples, pears and peaches taste delicious too!

Serves 2

For the caramelised apples
- 2 small apples, cored and diced
- ½ tsp cinnamon
- 1 tsp maple syrup

For the yogurt bowl
- 400g Greek yogurt (or non-dairy alternative)
- 60g granola (shop-bought is fine!) or oats
- 20g walnuts, chopped
- 0–2 tbsp honey, to taste

To caramelise the apples, combine the diced apples, cinnamon and maple syrup in a small pan along with 120ml of water. Bring to the boil and leave to simmer for about 5 minutes until the liquid has reduced and the apples are sticky and golden (you can do this in advance and store the caramelised apples in the fridge for 2–3 days to grab when you need them).

Divide the yogurt between two bowls and top with the granola and walnuts. Spoon over the caramelised apples and drizzle with honey, if using.

Smoked Salmon and Avocado Poke Bowl

'Poke bowls' have been a staple meal in Hawaii for centuries and provide comfort food and a nutritious meal at the same time – the perfect way to start the day! The Japanese also have a similar dish called 'chirashi', which means 'scattered' and is simply a bowl of rice, topped with raw fish, soy sauce and vegetables of your choice. Use the recipe below as a guide and experiment with different flavours (I often make a poke bowl out of whatever leftovers I have in my fridge!). And, if you're interested, it's pronounced 'poh-keh'!

Serves 2

- 250g cooked white or brown rice (about 100g dried weight or use a packet of microwave rice)
- 1 avocado, sliced
- 100g smoked salmon
- a handful of spinach or seaweed (you can find dried seaweed in the sushi aisle at most supermarkets, which then just needs rehydrating in cold water)
- 2 tbsp sesame seeds
- 1–2 tbsp soy sauce, to taste
- juice of 1 lime

Reheat the cooked rice as per the instructions on page 74.

Once heated, divide the rice between two bowls and top with the avocado, smoked salmon and spinach or seaweed.

Sprinkle with sesame seeds and drizzle over the soy sauce and lime juice before serving.

Beetroot Boiled Eggs

Boiled eggs are a great source of nutrients but they can be a bit boring. Beetroot not only adds a delicious sweet and earthy flavour but also makes the prettiest eggs you will have ever eaten! These eggs were inspired by the traditional spice-marinated 'nitamago' eggs you get with ramen in Japan, but I wanted to give them a purple twist. They last about a week in the fridge so you can make a batch of these at the weekend and grab a couple out of the fridge each morning.

Makes 4 servings

- 200g pickled beetroot, diced
- 1 tbsp caster sugar
- 100ml apple cider vinegar
- 8 boiled eggs, peeled (boil for 4–10 minutes depending on whether you prefer your eggs runny or hard-boiled)

Combine the beetroot, sugar and apple cider vinegar in a saucepan with 100ml of water and heat until it comes to the boil. Simmer for 5 minutes and leave to cool slightly.

Place the boiled eggs in a heatproof airtight container and pour the beetroot mixture over them. Top up the container with cold water if needed so the eggs are completely covered by the purple liquid. Leave to cool, cover and store in the fridge for at least 12 hours so the eggs absorb the flavours.

Serve with 2 slices of toasted Seedy Soda Bread (page 182) or Sweet Potato Rostis (page 171).

If you don't like the taste of pickled beetroot then you can get raw beetroot at farmers' markets, greengrocers and supermarkets. Simply trim the stalks, wash, wrap in foil and bake at 190°C for 45–55 minutes until the beetroot is tender. Leave to cool, peel, slice and use in place of the pickled beetroot.

Sun-dried Tomato and Spinach Scrambled Eggs-in-a-Jar

Scrambled eggs have been a long-time favourite of mine, but the thought of cooking them and washing-up pans afterwards always puts me off making them on weekday mornings. Making them in a jar or microwaveable airtight container is quick, easy and saves on the washing-up! The sun-dried tomatoes give a lovely Mediterranean vibe and adding spinach is a simple way to get more vegetables into your diet.

Serves 1

- 3–4 sun-dried tomatoes, sliced
- a handful of spinach, chopped
- 2 eggs
- 1 tbsp milk
- ¼ tsp salt
- black pepper, to taste
- 2 slices of toast (such as toasted Seedy Soda Bread, page 182), to serve

Soak the sun-dried tomatoes in boiling water for 5 minutes until they have softened a little.

Place the sun-dried tomatoes and spinach in a small/medium-sized jar (a jam jar works perfectly) or microwaveable airtight container. Crack in the eggs, add the milk and season with salt and pepper. Shake for 30 seconds until the mixture has combined.

Remove the lid and microwave on medium–high for 60 seconds. If the eggs are not cooked, continue to microwave for 15 seconds at a time until they are just set. Serve on top of two slices of toast.

Berry and Almond Breakfast Pizzas

If you want a quick, nutritious, family-friendly breakfast then these breakfast pizzas are ideal. They take less than five minutes to prepare and you can switch your toppings to please even the fussiest of eaters. As well as the recipe below, I love to top mine with sliced apples, walnuts and a drizzle of honey. And, if you fancy a different base for your breakfast pizza, then wraps, pancakes and waffles make a great alternative to pitta bread too.

Serves 2

- 2 large pitta breads
- 100g Greek yogurt, cream cheese or non-dairy alternative
- 150g mixed berries, fresh or defrosted from frozen
- 20g toasted flaked almonds
- 20g almond butter
- 0–2 tbsp honey or maple syrup, to taste

Toast the pitta breads for 2–3 minutes before spreading with yogurt or cream cheese so you have a thick layer covering the entire pitta.

Divide the berries between the pitta breads, sprinkle with flaked almonds and drizzle with almond butter. Add honey or maple syrup to sweeten before serving.

No-Bake Coconut and Almond Breakfast Bars

These breakfast bars are gooey, sticky, natural, wholesome and oh-so-delicious! They last at least a week in the fridge so I often make a batch on Sundays for mornings when I need a grab-and-go breakfast. I've used almond butter in the recipe but feel free to play around and use peanut butter, cashew butter or tahini if you prefer.

Makes 8–10 bars

- 200g oats
- 50g desiccated coconut, plus 2 tbsp extra for topping
- ½ tsp cinnamon
- ½ tsp salt
- 200g almond butter
- 4–5 tbsp runny honey or maple syrup
- 1 tsp vanilla extract
- 2 tbsp flaked almonds

Combine the oats, 50g of the desiccated coconut, the cinnamon and salt in a large bowl and set aside.

Place the almond butter, honey or maple syrup and vanilla extract in a small saucepan over a low heat and stir gently until the almond butter has melted.

Pour the almond butter mixture into the oat mixture and stir to combine. The mixture should be thick and sticky; if it is a little dry then add some water, one tablespoon at a time, until it comes together.

Lay out a large sheet of cling film or baking paper and empty the mixture into the middle of the sheet. Loosely wrap the cling film or baking paper around the mixture to prevent your hands from getting sticky and mould the mixture into a long rectangular sausage shape that you can cut into 8–10 slices. Once shaped, unwrap and sprinkle on the remaining desiccated coconut and the flaked almonds. Rewrap tightly so the mixture keeps its shape.

Place in the fridge for at least two hours, slice into bars and store in an airtight container in the fridge for up to a week.

Cherry Bakewell Muesli

Crunchy, nutty and fruity, this is one of my favourite breakfasts when I'm in a rush in the morning. You can make up a big batch at the weekend, store it in an airtight container and serve it with milk or yogurt and some fresh berries for a quick weekday breakfast packed full of nutrients.

Makes 10 servings (about 50g each)

- 200g oats
- 100g spelt, barley or rye flakes (or use more oats)
- 100g dried cherries
- 50g almonds, chopped
- 50g toasted flaked almonds
- 25g sunflower seeds
- 1 tsp almond extract

Combine all the ingredients in a bowl, mix thoroughly and store in an airtight container in a cool, dry cupboard until you are ready to eat.

Lazy Weekend Brunches

You know the weekend is going to be a good one when it begins with a decent brunch! These recipes are full of flavour and nutrients and are great for enjoying with friends and family to start your weekend off right.

The Fear-Free Full English

Nothing says Sunday morning quite like a full English breakfast and a steaming hot mug of tea. The Fear-Free Full English gives a nutritious and delicious twist to the traditional 'fry-up', with the addition of hummus, avocado and sweet chilli sauce. Choose your favourite bread to serve alongside it and feel free to cook your eggs however you like them. I've given instructions for poached eggs, but mix it up with scrambled, boiled or fried eggs if you prefer.

Serves 4

- 8 eggs
- 1 tbsp olive oil
- 4 tomatoes, halved
- 100g button mushrooms, quartered
- 4 handfuls of spinach
- ½ tsp salt
- 8 slices of bread
- 200g hummus (shop-bought is fine)
- 200g avocado, mashed
- 8–10 basil leaves, torn
- Sweet Chilli Sauce, to taste (page 179)

Bring a pan of water to a gentle simmer. Crack one egg into a small dish, tip it gently into the water and leave to poach for 3–4 minutes. Remove with a slotted spoon and drain on kitchen paper. Repeat with the remaining eggs, poaching two or three at a time as you get more confident. Once poached, leave the eggs to one side for reheating later (if you're just making this recipe for one or two people there will be fewer eggs to cook so you can leave the egg poaching until after you've cooked the vegetables and do them all in one go).

Heat the oil in a large frying pan. Place the tomatoes in the pan, cut side down. Add the mushrooms and fry for 4–5 minutes, turning the tomatoes over after 3 minutes. Add the spinach to the pan with a splash of water for the final 2–3 minutes and cook until wilted. Season the vegetables with salt.

Toast the bread and bring a large pan of water to the boil. Gently add all the poached eggs to the boiling water for about 1 minute to heat through. Remove and place on kitchen paper to drain any excess water.

Spread half the toast with hummus and top the other half with the mashed avocado. Divide between four plates. Place a poached egg on each slice of toast and top with the vegetables evenly. Sprinkle over the torn basil leaves and drizzle with Sweet Chilli Sauce before serving.

Italian Baked Eggs

Sweet, gooey, creamy and packed full of protein and nutrients, this is the perfect dish to make if you're having friends round for brunch. I love making it in one big baking dish and then everyone can dip their bread in and really embrace the happiness that comes with eating together. You can also make them in individual dishes or ramekins if you prefer.

Serves 4

- 2 tbsp olive oil
- 2 garlic cloves, crushed
- 2 x 400g tins chopped tomatoes
- 1 tsp caster sugar
- ½ tsp salt
- ½ tsp black pepper
- ¼ tsp dried chilli flakes
- 1 tsp dried mixed herbs (for example, basil, thyme, oregano)
- 8 eggs
- 1 x 250g ball mozzarella, torn into small pieces
- Fresh bread, to serve

Preheat your oven to 200°C and oil four medium-sized ramekin dishes or one large ovenproof baking dish.

Heat the olive oil in a saucepan over a medium heat and add the garlic. Fry for 1–2 minutes before adding the tomatoes, sugar, salt, pepper, chilli flakes and herbs. Simmer for 10 minutes or until the sauce has thickened and pour into your ramekins or baking dish.

Crack two eggs into each ramekin on top of the sauce (or all eight into your baking dish if you are making one large dish) and top with the torn mozzarella. Bake for 10–12 minutes until the egg whites are cooked and the yolks are still runny.

Serve with fresh bread and get dipping!

Scrambled Tofu Tacos

Scrambled tofu is a nutritious and delicious alternative if you fancy something a bit different to scrambled eggs. Tofu itself has a pretty neutral flavour so it absorbs the herbs and spices you cook it with – use the spice selection I've suggested here as a guide and play around with other combinations to suit your taste. I also love serving scrambled tofu with freshly toasted sourdough, wilted spinach and a sprinkling of toasted sunflower seeds.

Serves 4

- 1 tbsp olive oil
- 4 garlic cloves, crushed
- 1 onion, thinly sliced
- 1 head broccoli, cut into florets
- 1 red pepper, thinly sliced
- 1 x 400g block firm tofu, drained
- 2 tsp chilli powder
- 2 tsp cumin
- 2 tsp oregano
- 1 tsp turmeric
- 1 medium carrot, grated
- juice of ½ lemon
- 4 tortillas or wraps

Heat the oil in a large frying pan and add the garlic and onion. Cook for 3–4 minutes until the onion is translucent.

Add the broccoli and pepper and cook for another 3 minutes, stirring occasionally, before crumbling the tofu into the pan.

Mix together the chilli powder, cumin, oregano and turmeric with two to three tablespoons of water to form a smooth paste and then pour into the pan. Stir to coat everything in the pan with the spice mixture and cook for 3–4 minutes.

Add the grated carrot and lemon juice. Cook for another 3–4 minutes until the tofu is golden, stirring regularly. Divide the scrambled tofu between the tortillas or wraps and enjoy!

Japanese Pancakes

These vegetable-packed pancakes are inspired by a dish from Okinawa called 'hirayachi'. It's also called 'okonomiyaki' in mainland Japan, derived from the word 'okonomi', which means 'what you like'. This describes the dish pretty well – just fill your pancake mix with whatever vegetables you like and you have a tasty, easy-to-cook and nutrient-packed meal. I love serving it with traditional ingredients like sesame seeds and seaweed (most supermarkets now stock a huge array of Japanese ingredients that are fun to experiment with).

Serves 4

- 150g plain flour
- ¼ tsp baking powder
- ¼ tsp salt
- 4 eggs
- 100g potato, peeled and grated
- 400g red or white cabbage (about ½ a medium-sized cabbage), finely sliced
- 1 medium carrot, grated
- 10 spring onions, finely chopped
- 2 tsp grated fresh ginger
- 1 tbsp toasted sesame oil

Mix together the flour, baking powder, salt, eggs and 180ml of water in a large jug until there are no lumps.

Stir in the potatoes, cabbage, carrot, spring onions and ginger. The mixture should be very thick. Don't worry if it looks like there isn't enough pancake mixture to cover the vegetables – there is!

Heat the oil in a small frying pan and pour in a quarter of the mixture. Fry for 5–6 minutes on each side and repeat with the remaining mixture keeping the pancakes you've already made warm in a preheated oven.

Smoked Salmon Breakfast Pizzas

Smoked salmon bagels are a long-time favourite of mine and these breakfast pizzas take the traditional smoked salmon and soft cheese combo to a whole new level. They look impressive, taste amazing, are full of healthy fats, take less than 15 minutes to make and there is barely any washing-up – perfect for a lazy Sunday breakfast!

Serves 4

- 4 wraps, tortillas or Soccas (page 188)
- 60g pesto
- 250g ricotta
- 16 cherry tomatoes, halved
- 4 eggs
- 150g smoked salmon, sliced
- juice of ½ a lemon
- 4 handfuls of rocket

Preheat the oven to 180°C and place the wraps on a large baking tray.

Divide the pesto among the wraps and spread evenly. Spoon the ricotta in the middle of each wrap and top with the cherry tomatoes.

Crack an egg into the centre of each wrap (the ricotta and tomatoes should act like a wall to stop the egg white running over the edges of the wrap) and bake for 8–10 minutes until the egg whites are set.

Remove from the oven, top with the smoked salmon and a drizzle of lemon juice, and serve with a handful of rocket scattered over each one.

Lemon Ricotta Pancakes

Lemon and ricotta is a classic Italian flavour combination and when I went to Sardinia, I enjoyed it in all sorts of treats like cakes, tarts and pastries. It may seem weird to add cheese to pancakes but trust me, as well as creating a protein-rich breakfast, these will be the fluffiest pancakes you have ever eaten!

Serves 6
(makes around 30 pancakes)

- 90g plain flour
- 2 tsp baking powder
- ½ tsp cinnamon
- 30g caster sugar
- ¼ tsp salt
- 250g ricotta
- 2 large eggs, beaten
- 150ml milk
- zest and juice of 1 lemon
- 1–2 tbsp butter or coconut oil, for frying
- lemon curd, honey and fresh berries, to serve

Sift the flour, baking powder, cinnamon, sugar and salt into a bowl and place to one side.

Mix together the ricotta, eggs, milk, lemon zest and juice in a jug. Add the wet ingredients to the dry ingredients and mix until smooth.

Heat a little butter or oil in a large frying pan on a medium heat and pour in 4–5 large spoonfuls of the batter (one spoonful per pancake), making sure you leave enough room for them to spread out a little as they cook (they will be 8–12cm in diameter once cooked). Cook for 2–3 minutes until they have puffed up and you can see air bubbles in the pancakes, flip and cook for another 1–2 minutes.

Repeat with the remaining mixture and serve with lemon curd, honey and fresh berries.

Blueberry Breakfast Crepes

Crepes remind me of trips to France with my dad so these are a favourite of mine whenever I'm feeling nostalgic. I've used blueberries in the syrup but feel free to use your favourite berry or mix up the fillings with other flavour combos – caramelised apples (page 82), cinnamon and almond butter are perfect for chilly winter mornings.

Serves 4 (makes 8–10 crepes depending on thickness)

For the syrup
- 300g blueberries, fresh or frozen and defrosted
- 2 tbsp light brown sugar

For the crepes
- 200g plain flour
- 6 large eggs
- 350ml milk
- 1 tbsp caster sugar
- 1 tsp vanilla extract
- 1–2 tbsp butter or oil, for frying

Try serving with Greek yogurt and fresh berries.

Begin by making the blueberry syrup. Place the blueberries and sugar in a small saucepan with 100ml water. Bring to a boil and simmer for 8–10 minutes, stirring occasionally, until the syrup is thick and sticky.

While the syrup is cooking, preheat the oven to 120°C and make the crepe batter by combining the crepe ingredients in a jug with 150ml of water and mixing until smooth.

Heat a lightly oiled medium-sized frying pan over a low heat and add about 60ml (three tablespoons) of the batter to the pan. Swirl gently so you get a thin coating of batter over the base of the pan and cook for 2–3 minutes until the crepe is stable enough to flip.

Use a spatula to turn the crepe over (or you can try flipping it in the air!) and cook on the other side for 1–2 minutes. Repeat with the remaining batter, keeping the crepes you've already made warm in a preheated oven.

Remove the crepes from the oven, fill each one with one or two tablespoons of Greek yogurt, drizzle over the blueberry syrup and wrap or roll.

Chocolate Peanut Butter Baked Oatmeal

Gooey, nutty, chocolatey and comforting, this is kind of like eating dessert for breakfast! It's packed full of energising ingredients, like oats and peanut butter, and goes perfectly with sliced banana or fresh berries for extra sweetness and nutrients. If you want more of a protein-rich meal, then just add a couple of scoops of chocolate-flavoured protein powder and a little extra milk or water before baking.

Serves 4

- 180g oats
- 25g cocoa powder
- 1 tsp baking powder
- 1 tsp cinnamon
- ½ tsp salt
- 350ml milk
- 1 egg, beaten
- 60g peanut butter (smooth or crunchy), melted
- 2–3 tbsp runny honey, to taste
- Greek yogurt and fruit, to serve

Try optional extras, such as walnuts, raisins or cacao nibs.

Preheat the oven to 180°C and grease a medium-sized baking dish or four individual ramekins.

Combine the oats, cocoa powder, baking powder, cinnamon and salt in a bowl and leave to one side.

In another bowl, mix together the milk, egg, peanut butter and honey and then pour into the dry ingredients. Mix well and stir in any extras you are using.

Pour into your prepared dish or ramekins and bake in the oven for 15–20 minutes depending on the size of the dish you are using. You want the oatmeal to bounce back if you push your finger gently into the top.

Serve warm with Greek yogurt and fruit.

Coconut, Raspberry and Pomegranate Rice Porridge

I fell in love with the flavours of coconut rice porridge when I was studying Ayurvedic nutrition and was struggling with my digestion. Basmati rice is one of the easiest things to digest and has been used for centuries in Asian cultures for anyone who suffers from wind, bloating and indigestion. Soaking the rice before cooking not only makes it easier to digest, but gives you a beautifully sweet flavour and a creamy texture that is perfect for a nourishing family breakfast.

Serves 4

- 250g basmati rice
- ¼ tsp salt
- 200ml tinned coconut milk
- ½ tsp cinnamon
- 0–2 tbsp runny honey or maple syrup, to taste
- 60g mixed nuts, chopped
- 150g raspberries, fresh or frozen and defrosted
- 50g pomegranate seeds, fresh or frozen and defrosted

Rinse the rice and leave to soak in cold water for 20 minutes to soften before draining and rinsing again.

Bring a large pan of water to the boil and add the soaked rice and salt. Cook for 10 minutes, drain and place back in the pan.

Add in the coconut milk, cinnamon, honey or maple syrup, nuts and half the raspberries and pomegranate seeds. Heat on low for 2–3 minutes until warmed through.

Divide the mixture between four bowls and top with the remaining raspberries and pomegranate seeds, adding an extra drizzle of honey or maple syrup if you like.

If using a fresh pomegranate, simply cut it in half, turn it sliced side down and tap it firmly with the back of a spoon to get the seeds out.

Lunchbox Ideas

As well as being delicious and nutritious, these recipes are quick and easy to make and are perfect for popping in your bag to take to work with you. Simply make them the night before and store them in the fridge overnight. And, if you can make time to eat them away from your desk without checking social media or trying to multitask, then you'll probably enjoy them even more. Plus, research suggests that making the time for a lunch break can help you feel less tired and be more productive!

Sweet Moroccan Falafel

I eat beans and legumes regularly because they are rich in vitamins, minerals and fibre – and falafel are a simple and tasty way to eat them. If you find beans make you bloated or give you wind, then try adding a pinch of kelp powder to the recipe or eating them with seaweed (this is an ancient Japanese tip for reducing the wind-causing qualities of beans!).

Serves 2 (makes 12 falafel)

For the falafel
- 40g dried apricots, chopped
- 30g dates, pitted and chopped
- 1 x 400g tin chickpeas, drained (240g drained weight)
- 2 garlic cloves, crushed
- ½ onion, diced
- ½ red pepper, diced
- 1 tsp dried coriander
- 1 tsp cumin
- ½ tsp cinnamon
- ½ tsp chilli flakes
- ½ tsp baking powder
- 2–4 tbsp plain flour

Preheat the oven to 180°C. Soak the apricots and dates in boiling water for 5 minutes.

Place the soaked fruit and all the other falafel ingredients, except the flour, into a food processor and blend until crumbly.

Add the flour one tablespoon at a time until you can mould the mixture without it sticking to your hands.

Shape the mixture into falafel balls (about 30g each), arrange on a lightly oiled baking tray and bake in the oven for 15–25 minutes. The longer you bake them, the crispier they will be.

Pop the falafel on a plate or in a lunchbox with some Courgette Coins or other roasted vegetables. Add a drizzle of Yogurt and Mustard Dressing before serving.

Serve with Roasted Courgette Coins (page 176) or other roasted vegetables, with a drizzle of Yogurt and Mustard Dressing (page 178).

Greek Frittata

Frittatas are a great way to use up any leftover vegetables you have in the fridge. This recipe is inspired by Mediterranean flavours and ingredients – tomatoes, olives and feta – which give it a lovely summery vibe. Grating courgette into the frittata is a simple way to get more vegetables into your meal and makes a beautifully big lunchtime frittata that will keep you full until dinner.

Serves 2

- 4 sun-dried tomatoes, sliced
- 1 tbsp olive oil
- ½ red onion, diced
- 1 courgette, grated
- 80g cherry tomatoes, halved
- 100g spinach
- 6 eggs, beaten
- 25g black olives, pitted and diced
- 1 tsp dried mixed herbs
- ½ tsp salt
- 50g feta

Heat the grill to medium. Soak the sun-dried tomatoes in boiling water for 5 minutes until they have softened a little.

Heat the oil in a medium-sized frying pan and add the onion, courgette and cherry tomatoes. Fry for 2–3 minutes. Add the spinach with a splash of water and fry for another 1–2 minutes until the spinach has wilted.

In a jug, combine the eggs, sun-dried tomatoes, olives, herbs and salt with two tablespoons of water and mix well.

Pour the egg mixture into the frying pan and cook for 3–4 minutes until the top of the frittata is just beginning to set.

Crumble over the feta, transfer the frittata to the grill (keeping the frying pan handle away from direct heat) and cook for 6–8 minutes until the eggs are set and the frittata has puffed up slightly.

Leave to cool, cut into quarters and pop two wedges per person into a lunchbox with a handful of salad and store in the fridge overnight.

Rainbow Sandwich

Soggy bread and lacklustre fillings have given sandwiches a bad rep, but this recipe will reignite your passion for them with its beautiful colours, tasty flavours and energising five-vegetable filling. I often make up a big batch of the chickpea filling and add it to bread and wraps throughout the week.

Serves 1

- ½ x 400g tin chickpeas, drained (120g drained weight)
- 1 tbsp natural yogurt
- 1 tsp yellow mustard
- ¼ tsp turmeric
- ¼ tsp salt
- 2 slices bread
- 1 tsp butter or other spread (hummus also works beautifully here)
- ½ carrot, grated
- ¼ yellow pepper, sliced
- 40g red cabbage, sliced
- a handful of spinach
- 1 tomato, sliced

Prepare the chickpea filling by placing the chickpeas in a bowl with the yogurt, mustard, turmeric and salt. Mash with a fork until the chickpeas are crushed and golden yellow in colour and set aside.

Spread the bread with butter or other spread, top one slice with the chickpea filling and layer up the vegetables and tomato slices. Top with the other slice of bread, pressing down slightly to help secure the filling. Wrap in greaseproof paper and place in a lunchbox.

Sushi Jar

This is the perfect lunch if you love sushi but don't want the hassle of making it or the expense of buying it ready-made. I usually cook up a big batch of rice and make up a few different dressings (see page 178) at the weekend. This means that lunches like this only take a matter of minutes to prepare. If you're struggling to find seaweed (nori) in the supermarket then look in the Asian aisle – you'll usually find it dried in sheets.

Serves 2

- 1 tbsp sesame oil
- 80g shelled edamame beans (fresh or frozen)
- 250g cooked rice (about 100g dried weight or you can use 1 pack of microwave rice here)
- 2 tbsp soy sauce or Soy and Ginger Dressing (page 178)
- 1 seaweed sheet (nori), cut into thin strips (optional)
- 4 spring onions, chopped
- 1 carrot, grated
- 1 avocado, diced
- ½ cucumber, cut into thin matchsticks
- 100g smoked salmon, tinned crab meat or tinned tuna
- juice of ½ lime
- wasabi paste, to taste (optional)

Heat sesame oil in a small frying pan or wok and add edamame beans. Stir-fry for 3–4 minutes and leave to cool slightly.

Place the rice in a bowl and pour over the soy sauce or dressing. Mix well until the rice is well coated.

Layer all the ingredients, except the lime juice and wasabi paste, in any order you like in a jar or airtight container. Squeeze over the lime juice and top with a little wasabi paste, if using. Leave in the fridge overnight and just grab in the morning.

Chickpea and Coconut Soup

Simple, quick, subtly spiced and super-satisfying, this soup is perfect for when you want something nourishing and comforting for lunch but don't have much time to prepare anything in advance. You can make the whole dish in less than 10 minutes and it goes perfectly with a chunk of Seedy Soda Bread (page 182).

Serves 2

- 2 tbsp olive oil
- 4 garlic cloves, crushed
- ½ tsp dried chilli flakes
- 1 x 400g tin chickpeas, drained (240g drained weight)
- 200ml tinned coconut milk
- 400ml vegetable stock
- ½ tsp smoked paprika
- juice of ½ lemon
- salt and pepper
- few mint leaves, chopped

Heat the oil in a large saucepan over a medium heat. Add the garlic and chilli flakes and fry for 1–2 minutes.

Set aside two tablespoons of chickpeas and add the rest to the saucepan. Mix and fry for another minute.

Pour in the coconut milk, reserving 2 tablespoons to garnish, with the stock and add in the paprika. Season to taste and simmer for 2–3 minutes.

Either pour into a blender or use a hand blender to blend the soup until thick and smooth. Season to taste, then stir in the lemon juice and the remaining chickpeas. Swirl through the reserved coconut milk and scatter over the chopped mint leaves. Divide between two bowls, if you're eating the soup immediately, or between two microwaveable containers, ready to take to work and reheat. Leave to cool and store in the fridge if you're planning to eat it the next day.

Spicy Sweetcorn Soup

This is the perfect combination of spicy and sweet. Feel free to add more vegetables, such as carrots, peas and green beans, to add texture, make the soup even heartier and boost the nutrients.

Serves 2

- 1 tbsp olive oil
- 1 small onion, diced
- 2 garlic cloves, crushed
- ½ red pepper, diced
- 1 tsp grated fresh ginger
- 250g sweetcorn, tinned (drained) or frozen and defrosted
- ½ tsp chilli flakes
- ½ tsp turmeric
- 1 tsp cumin
- 1 tsp fresh coriander, chopped
- 125g cooked rice (about 50g dried weight or half a pack of microwave rice)
- salt and pepper

Heat the oil in a large saucepan and add the onion and garlic. Cook for 2–3 minutes before adding the red pepper and ginger. Fry for another 1–2 minutes.

Add the sweetcorn to the pan along with the rest of the spices and coriander, and stir.

Add just enough water to cover the sweetcorn (about 400–500ml) and simmer for 5 minutes.

Either pour into a blender or use a hand blender to blend the soup until smooth. Season to taste, stir in the rice, and either heat for another 2–3 minutes if eating immediately or take off the heat if you're making the soup in advance. Divide between two bowls, if you're eating the soup immediately, or between two microwaveable containers, ready to reheat when you want to eat it. Leave to cool and store in the fridge if you're planning to eat it the next day.

Super-Simple Chilli

Beans work beautifully with spicy, smoky sauces and this chilli is perfect for winter lunchtimes when you need something warm and comforting. The beans are a great source of protein and fibre and adding avocado just before eating adds a velvety creaminess to the chilli as well as giving you a dose of healthy fat.

Serves 2

- 1 tbsp olive oil
- 2 garlic cloves, crushed
- ½ red onion, diced
- ½ red pepper, diced
- 1 x 400g tin mixed beans, drained
- 1 x 400g tin chopped tomatoes
- 1 tsp chilli powder
- 1 tsp smoked paprika
- ½ tsp cumin
- ½ tsp caster sugar
- ½ tsp salt
- 80g sweetcorn, tinned (drained) or frozen and defrosted
- 1 avocado, sliced

Preheat the oven to 140°C. Heat the oil in a small frying pan. Add the garlic, onion and pepper and fry for 2–3 minutes.

Empty the beans into a large bowl. Pour off about half the liquid from the tinned tomatoes and discard. Add the remaining contents of the tin to the bowl with the spices, sugar, salt and sweetcorn. Mix well and empty into a medium-sized baking or casserole dish and bake in the oven for 20–30 minutes until bubbling.

Leave to cool, divide between two airtight containers and pop in the fridge overnight. You can eat this cold or, if you prefer it warm, just reheat in the microwave for a couple of minutes before topping with avocado just before eating.

Try serving with rice, Greek yogurt and fresh coriander for a more filling lunch.

Almond and Apricot Couscous with Mini Meatballs

Couscous is a great ingredient because it is so versatile and you can jazz it up with all kinds of flavours. It goes perfectly with these pork meatballs and a drizzle of yogurt. If you don't eat meat, then simply replace the meatballs with Sweet Moroccan Falafel (page 108). Add some roasted vegetables (page 176) or a simple side salad for extra nutrients.

Serves 2

For the mini meatballs
- 150g pork mince
- 30g dried apricots, chopped
- ½ tsp dried sage
- 1 tsp chilli flakes
- ½ tsp salt
- 1 tbsp olive oil

For the couscous
- 120g couscous (dried weight)
- 240ml boiling water
- 6 spring onions, sliced
- 30g dried apricots, chopped
- 20g almonds, chopped
- juice of ½ lime
- 1 tbsp olive oil
- ½ tsp salt
- ½ tsp black pepper
- 4 tbsp natural yogurt

Make the meatballs by combining the mince, apricots, sage, chilli flakes and salt in a bowl and stir to combine. Shape the mixture into 6–8 little meatballs using your hands.

Heat the oil in a small frying pan over medium heat and fry the meatballs for 6–8 minutes until golden, stirring occasionally.

While the meatballs are cooking, place the couscous in a heat-proof bowl and add the boiling water. Cover and set aside for 10 minutes.

Fluff the couscous up with a fork, add the remaining ingredients (except the yogurt), mix well and divide between two airtight containers. Top with the meatballs and leave to cool before storing in the fridge overnight. Drizzle over the yogurt before serving.

Simple Salads

Salads make perfect lunches or mid-week dinners and these recipes are packed full of nutrients and flavour. They're inspired by ingredients from all over the world and have a real summery vibe!

Mexican Tuna Bean Salad with Tortilla Chips

This is a great store cupboard meal for when you're running short on fresh ingredients. It's always handy to have a couple of tins of tuna and mixed beans in stock because they are both so versatile. Tuna is packed full of protein and beans are a great source of fibre. I love to spice them up with chilli but if you're not a fan of spicy food then just switch the chilli for some sliced red pepper for a bit of sweetness.

Serves 2

- 2 tortillas (corn tortillas work best)
- 1 x 185g tin tuna, drained
- ½ x 400g tin mixed beans, drained (about 120g drained weight)
- 1 head Little Gem or romaine lettuce (about 150g), chopped
- 2 tomatoes, diced
- 1 avocado, diced
- 1 red chilli, deseeded and finely sliced
- ½ red onion, diced
- juice of 1 lime
- ½ tsp salt
- 2 tbsp olive oil
- 30g hard cheese, grated (for example, queso blanco, Monterey Jack)
- 2 tbsp fresh coriander, chopped
- 2 tbsp sour cream

Preheat the oven to 180°C and slice each tortilla into 8 triangles. Arrange on a baking tray and cook for 5–6 minutes on each side until just beginning to brown.

While the tortillas are cooking, combine the tuna, beans, lettuce, tomatoes, avocado, chilli and onion in a bowl and toss in the lime juice, salt and olive oil to coat.

Divide the salad mixture between two plates, sprinkle over the cheese and coriander and add one tablespoon of sour cream per serving. Serve with the tortilla chips.

Smoked Mackerel and Beetroot Salad

I didn't think I liked smoked mackerel or beetroot before I experimented with this salad! This proves that when you let go of restrictive food rules, explore new foods and play around with flavours, you open up a whole new world of tasty and nutritious meals.

Serves 2

- 170g green beans, fresh or frozen and defrosted
- 170g broccoli, cut into florets
- 4 large handfuls of spinach
- 100g pickled beetroot, diced into pea-sized cubes (if you don't like pickled beetroot then you can bake your own – see page 86)
- 4 small smoked mackerel fillets (160g–200g in total)
- 2 tsp mixed seeds
- a drizzle of Yogurt and Mustard Dressing (page 178)

Bring a large pan of salted water to the boil and add the green beans and broccoli. Cook for 4–5 minutes until tender. Once cooked, drain and rinse under cold water.

Divide the spinach between two plates and top with the green beans, broccoli and beetroot. Add two mackerel fillets per plate, sprinkle over the seeds and drizzle with Yogurt and Mustard Dressing before serving.

Rice Noodle Salad with Ginger Sesame Tofu

I first had tofu while I was training to be a yoga teacher in Thailand and every time I eat it, it takes me right back to my time in such a beautiful country. Tofu is a great plant-based source of protein and works like a sponge to absorb the spicy marinade in this recipe. If you don't have rice noodles to hand then feel free to use brown or basmati rice instead.

Serves 2

For the tofu
- 50ml soy sauce
- 1 tbsp toasted sesame oil
- 1 tbsp grated fresh ginger
- 2 garlic cloves, crushed
- 1 tsp chilli flakes
- juice of ½ lime
- 1 x 400g block firm tofu, drained and cut into small cubes

For the salad
- 200g dried rice noodles (dried weight)
- 4 handfuls of lettuce, chopped
- 2 carrots, sliced into matchsticks
- 1 cucumber, sliced into matchsticks
- 4 tbsp sesame seeds
- a drizzle of Soy and Ginger Dressing (page 178)

Make the tofu marinade by combining the soy sauce, sesame oil, ginger, garlic, chilli flakes and lime juice in a bowl. Add the cubed tofu and cover with the marinade. Leave in the fridge for as long as possible, ideally overnight (it's still delicious to cook with straight away but the flavour won't be as strong).

Preheat the oven to 200°C and grease a baking tray. Remove the tofu from the marinade and spread out evenly on the prepared tray. Bake in the oven for 15 minutes then drizzle over some of the leftover marinade and shake the tofu around. Bake for another 10 minutes. Add more marinade and bake for another 5 minutes (around 30 minutes in total).

While the tofu is baking, cook the noodles according to the packet instructions and rinse under cold water once they're cooked.

Divide the noodles between two plates, arrange the vegetables around the outside, top with the tofu and sesame seeds, and drizzle over the dressing.

Asian Pulled Chicken Salad

This super-easy-to-make Asian salad is packed full of zingy flavours, crunchy vegetables and a bit of spice too. Feel free to swap the chicken for your favourite protein-rich food – beef works really well if you're a meat eater and, if you're not, then tofu is a great alternative.

Serves 2

- 2 cooked chicken breasts, diced or shredded (page 75) or baked tofu (page 128)
- 100g edamame beans (fresh or frozen)
- 2 carrots, grated
- ½ cucumber, sliced into matchsticks
- 4 spring onions, sliced
- ½ red cabbage (about 150g), shredded
- ½ red pepper, finely sliced
- 1 red chilli, finely sliced
- 250g cooked rice (about 100g dried weight or you can use 1 pack of microwave rice here)
- 25g cashews, crushed
- 2 tbsp fresh coriander, chopped
- a drizzle of Soy and Ginger Dressing (page 178)

Combine all the ingredients, except the cashews and coriander, in a bowl and mix well.

Divide between two dishes, top with the cashews and coriander and drizzle with the dressing before serving.

Eight-Ingredient Mediterranean Pasta Salad

This super simple salad is made up of some of the most traditional foods and flavours found in Ikaria and the Greek islands – feta, olives and tomatoes. Eating it reminds me of my family holidays in Crete as a kid. And that's what food should do: bring back happy memories so you're not only getting healthier by feeding your body nutritious foods, you're getting happier too.

Serves 2

- 120g farfalle or pasta of your choice (there's a simple recipe for homemade pasta on page 175)
- 8 sun-dried tomatoes, sliced
- ½ cucumber, diced
- 100g cherry tomatoes, halved
- ½ red onion, finely sliced
- 25g black olives, pitted and chopped
- 100g feta
- a handful of fresh basil, torn
- a drizzle of Lemon and Herb Vinaigrette (page 178)
- salt and pepper

Bring a large pan of water to the boil and cook the pasta according to the packet instructions (usually 8–12 minutes). Drain and rinse under cold water.

Soak the sun-dried tomatoes in boiling water for 5 minutes until they have softened a little.

Combine the pasta, sun-dried tomatoes, cucumber, cherry tomatoes, onion and olives in a large bowl and mix well. Season to taste.

Crumble over the feta, sprinkle the basil leaves on top and drizzle with the vinaigrette before serving.

Spiced Chickpea Salad

This salad is so easy to rustle up and, as well as working well as a meal in itself, it's great as a side and perfect for popping in a lunchbox and taking to work if you have any left over.

Serves 2

For the chickpeas
- 1 tbsp olive oil
- 1 x 400g tin chickpeas, drained (240g drained weight)
- juice of ½ lemon
- 1 tsp soy sauce
- 1 garlic clove, crushed
- 2 tsp smoked paprika
- 1 tsp cumin
- ¼ tsp chilli flakes
- a pinch of sugar

For the salad
- 1 cucumber, diced
- 1 red pepper, diced
- 4 tomatoes, diced
- 2 tbsp fresh parsley, chopped
- a drizzle of Lemon and Tahini Dressing (page 178), to serve
- 2 warmed pitta breads, to serve

To cook the chickpeas, heat the oil in a medium frying pan and add the chickpeas. Fry for 3–4 minutes until they start to pop.

While the chickpeas are cooking, combine the lemon juice, soy sauce, garlic, spices and sugar (I find the easiest way to do this is to put them all in a small jar and give them a shake) and pour into the pan. Stir and cook for another 1–2 minutes.

Once the chickpeas are cooked, transfer to a bowl, combine with the salad ingredients and mix well. Divide between two plates, drizzle over the dressing and serve with a pitta bread each.

Lentil Salad with Goat's Cheese and Walnuts

This salad goes to show that you can create a meal in a matter of minutes without compromising nutrition or taste – the earthiness of lentils goes perfectly with the soft, creaminess of goat's cheese and the sweetness of honey. Lentils are one of the most nutrient-dense legumes and a great source of plant-based protein. They're packed full of fibre and rich in probiotics, which help keep your gut healthy.

Serves 2

- 1 x 400g tin green lentils, drained and rinsed (240g drained weight)
- ½ red onion, diced
- 100g cherry tomatoes, quartered
- 1 carrot, finely diced into pea-sized cubes
- 80g mixed salad leaves
- 25g raisins
- 25g walnuts, chopped
- 1 tsp mustard (smooth or wholegrain)
- 1 tsp runny honey
- juice of ½ lemon
- 2 tbsp olive oil
- ½ tsp salt
- 2 tbsp fresh herbs of your choice, chopped
- 100g goat's cheese

Combine all the ingredients, except the goat's cheese, in a bowl and mix well.

Divide the salad between two dishes and crumble the cheese on top before serving.

Halloumi, Butternut Squash and Quinoa Salad

Salty, sweet and spicy, this is the perfect salad for when you fancy something healthy, hearty and rustic. It's packed full of nutrients too – quinoa is a great source of protein and carbohydrates; halloumi gives you a healthy dose of fat; and butternut squash is full of vitamins.

Serves 2

- 90g quinoa (dried weight or you can use 1 pack of ready-made quinoa, available in most supermarkets)
- ¼ tsp salt
- ½ small butternut squash, peeled and cubed (you can also get diced and frozen butternut squash in most supermarkets)
- 2 tbsp olive oil
- ½ small red onion, sliced
- 1 garlic clove, crushed
- ½ tsp chilli flakes
- 150g kale
- 100g halloumi, sliced into eight pieces
- a drizzle of Sweet Chilli Sauce, homemade (page 179) or shop-bought

Rinse the quinoa and place in a saucepan with 250ml of water and the salt. Bring to the boil and simmer for 15–20 minutes until the quinoa is soft. Remove from the heat, cover and leave for 5 minutes.

While the quinoa is cooking, place the cubed butternut squash in a heatproof bowl and add two tablespoons of water. Cover and microwave for 5–8 minutes until the cubes are soft but not mushy. If you have more time then roasting the butternut squash will make it sweeter and nuttier (see box below).

While the butternut squash is cooking, heat one tablespoon of oil in a large saucepan and add the onion, garlic and chilli flakes. Fry for 2–3 minutes and add the kale along with two or three tablespoons of water. Stir-fry for 4 minutes and then add the butternut squash. Stir-fry for another 4 minutes until the kale is tender.

In a small frying pan heat the remaining oil and add the halloumi. Fry for 2 minutes on each side until it starts to go golden.

Add the cooked quinoa to the pan with the kale in and stir to combine. Divide the quinoa and kale mixture between two bowls, top with the halloumi and drizzle over the Sweet Chilli Sauce.

HOW TO ROAST BUTTERNUT SQUASH
Preheat the oven to 200°C. Peel the butternut squash, dice it into small cubes and toss with one tablespoon of olive oil and a little salt and pepper. Spread the butternut squash out evenly on a baking tray and roast for 30–40 minutes until the squash is tender and golden.

Two-Pot Egg, Pea and Potato Salad

Nothing says summer quite like a potato salad. Fresh, zingy and super-easy to make, this salad is perfect for speedy lunches, weekday dinners or picnics in the park. Feel free to add in more vegetables, such as green beans, broccoli and sweetcorn, for extra nutrients and flavour, and add a sprinkling of chilli flakes if you fancy a bit of spice.

Serves 2

- 400g baby new potatoes, halved
- 4 eggs
- 150g frozen peas
- 100g pea shoots or mixed salad leaves
- 2 tbsp olive oil
- juice of ½ lemon
- 30g Parmesan, grated
- salt and pepper

Place the new potatoes in a large saucepan of salted water and bring to the boil. Reduce to a simmer and leave for 15 minutes.

While the potatoes are cooking, place the eggs in a separate pan and bring to the boil. Simmer for 8 minutes. Once cooked, place the boiled eggs in a bowl of ice-cold water until cool enough to handle and then peel.

Once the potatoes have been boiling for about 15 minutes, add the peas to the pan and boil for another 2–3 minutes or until the potatoes are tender (they may need a little longer depending on the size of your potatoes).

Remove the pan from the heat and drain the potatoes and peas.

Combine the potatoes and peas with the mixed leaves in a large bowl and toss with the olive oil and lemon juice. Season to taste.

Divide the leaf and potato mixture between two dishes, quarter the eggs and place 8 quarters onto each plate. Sprinkle with the grated Parmesan before serving.

Speedy Midweek Suppers

On weekday evenings food needs to be quick and simple. These recipes are designed so you can have a tasty and nourishing meal and still have time to relax after a hard day at work.

Stuffed Aubergines with Feta, Raisins and Walnuts

This is a super simple and delicious vegetarian main which you can always prepare in advance and reheat if you're short on time. Feta, raisins and walnuts work beautifully with the earthiness of the aubergines, but feel free to play around with other fillings – I also love stuffing them with spicy rice and lentils to give the dish an Asian twist.

Serves 2

- 2 large aubergines, cut in half lengthways
- 2 tbsp olive oil
- 20g raisins
- ½ onion, finely sliced
- 1 tbsp dried parsley
- 100g feta, crumbled
- 50g walnuts, chopped
- zest and juice of ½ lemon
- salt and pepper

Serve with Spicy Sweet Potato Wedges (page 168) and a big green side salad.

Preheat the oven to 200°C. Score the aubergine flesh in a criss-cross fashion with a knife and drizzle over one tablespoon of the olive oil. Place on a baking tray and bake in the oven for 20–25 minutes until the flesh is soft.

While the aubergines are cooking, soak the raisins in a cup of boiling water for 5 minutes.

Heat the remaining olive oil in a pan. Add the onion and fry for 3–4 minutes. Stir in the parsley and then empty everything into a medium-sized bowl.

Drain the raisins and add them to the bowl along with the feta, walnuts and lemon zest and juice. Once the aubergines are cooked, scoop out the flesh, chop into small cubes and add it to the bowl with the rest of the ingredients. Season to taste, mix well and spoon back into the skins.

Return the aubergines to the oven for another 5–10 minutes or until the cheese has melted and the stuffing is gooey and golden.

Super-Quick Coconut and Peanut Stir-Fry

This is an incredibly easy stir-fry you can cook up in 15 minutes. It's full of exotic Thai flavours and reminds me of my travels in Chiang Mai when I was training as a yoga teacher. Simply choose beef, chicken or tofu and get stir-frying! You can make your own curry paste if you have time, but there is absolutely nothing wrong with going for a shop-bought option.

Serves 2

- 1 tbsp toasted sesame oil
- 1 garlic clove, crushed
- 1 tbsp grated fresh ginger
- 1 chilli, sliced
- 8 spring onions, finely sliced
- 2 tbsp Thai red curry paste
- 300g chicken breast or beef frying steak, thinly sliced, or 400g firm tofu, drained and cubed
- 100g mangetout
- 150g bean sprouts
- 200ml tinned coconut milk
- juice of ½ lime
- 30g peanuts (unsalted or salted), crushed
- 250g cooked rice or rice noodles, to serve (about 100g dried weight or a 250g pack of microwave rice or noodles)

Heat the oil in a large frying pan or wok over a medium heat and add the garlic, ginger, chilli and spring onions. Fry for 2–3 minutes and then add the curry paste and chicken, beef or tofu.

Stir-fry for another 5 minutes, stirring occasionally until the meat is starting to brown or tofu is beginning to colour and firm up.

Add the mangetout and bean sprouts and fry for another 2–3 minutes.

Stir in the coconut milk and simmer for 3–4 minutes until reduced slightly.

Divide the stir-fry between two bowls, squeeze over the lime juice, top with crushed peanuts and serve with rice or rice noodles.

Spicy Chickpea, Mushroom and Spinach Bake

Inspired by the flavours of Sardinia, this dish is perfect for when you're craving something hearty and healthy – baked beans for grown-ups! Chickpeas and mozzarella are full of protein and the tomatoes and spinach give you a good hit of vitamins. I love serving this with a chunk of Seedy Soda Bread (page 182) to mop up the sauce.

Serves 2

- 1 tbsp olive oil
- ½ red onion, finely sliced
- 1 garlic clove, crushed
- 1 tsp chilli flakes
- 100g mushrooms, sliced
- 1 x 400g tin chopped tomatoes
- ½ tsp dried oregano
- ½ tsp caster sugar
- 1 x 400g tin chickpeas, drained (about 240g drained weight)
- 100g spinach, chopped
- ½ x 125g ball mozzarella, torn
- salt and pepper

Preheat the oven to 180°C. Heat the oil in a frying pan over a medium heat. Add the onion and fry for 2–3 minutes before adding the garlic, chilli flakes and mushrooms. Fry for another 2–3 minutes.

Stir in the tomatoes and add the oregano and sugar. Bring to a simmer and cook for 4 minutes. Stir in the chickpeas and spinach and simmer until the spinach has wilted (around 1–2 minutes).

Pour the contents of the pan into a baking dish and scatter the mozzarella over the top. Season to taste and bake in the oven for 20 minutes until the sauce is bubbling and the mozzarella is gooey.

Mini Falafel Burgers

There is something about falafel that makes a simple midweek meal feel like a bit of a feast. You can easily double the recipe to give you extra falafel for lunch the following day. I love serving mine with hummus and a selection of sides depending on which vegetables I have to hand.

**Serves 2
(makes 12 mini burgers)**

- 1 x 400g tin chickpeas, drained (240g drained weight)
- 2 garlic cloves, crushed
- ½ onion, diced
- 1 tsp sesame seeds, plus extra for coating (optional)
- 1½ tsp cumin
- 1 tsp dried coriander
- ½ tsp chilli flakes
- ½ tsp baking powder
- 2–4 tbsp plain flour
- 1 tbsp olive oil
- salt and pepper

Place all the ingredients, except the flour and olive oil, into a food processor and pulse until you get a crumbly mixture. Season to taste.

Add in the flour one tablespoon at a time until you get a mixture you can shape with your hands without it being too sticky.

Shape one tablespoon of the mixture into a patty and roll in sesame seeds, if using. Repeat with the rest of the mixture. You should get 12 burgers weighing about 30g each.

Heat the oil in a large frying pan over a medium heat and fry for 3–4 minutes on each side. Serve warm.

Serving suggestion:
Spicy Sweet Potato Wedges (page 168) and Warm Brussels Sprout Slaw (page 172).

Super-Green Pasta

Nothing is quite as comforting as a steaming hot bowl of pasta. If you have a bit more time you can make your own pasta using the recipe on page 175. And feel free to top with cooked chicken or a couple of poached eggs if you want more protein-rich foods in your meal.

Serves 2

- 150g dried pasta
- ½ head broccoli, cut into small florets
- 80g frozen peas
- 80g frozen shelled edamame beans
- 4 handfuls of spinach, chopped
- 4 tbsp pesto
- 40g Parmesan, grated

Bring a large pan of salted water to the boil, add the pasta and cook for 5 minutes.

Add the broccoli, peas, edamame beans and spinach to the pan and cook for another 4–5 minutes until the pasta is al dente (still has a bit of a bite to it).

Once cooked, drain in a colander, reserving about 100ml of the cooking water, and return everything to the pan.

Add the pesto, the reserved cooking water and half the Parmesan and mix well. Divide between two dishes and sprinkle with the remaining Parmesan before serving.

Sardinian-Style Couscous with Cod, Almonds and Tomatoes

This is a lovely meal to cook mindfully to help you relax after a long day at work. It's full of Mediterranean flavours to please your taste buds and fresh, nutritious ingredients to nourish your body. Serve it with a big green salad or some roasted vegetables.

Serves 2

- 1 tbsp olive oil
- 1 onion, finely sliced
- 1 x 400g tin chopped tomatoes
- ½ tsp caster sugar
- ½ tsp dried oregano or thyme
- 500ml vegetable stock
- 125g couscous (dried weight)
- 100ml boiling water
- ¼ tsp cinnamon
- 2 cod fillets (125–150g each), cut into 5cm cubes
- 25g black olives, pitted and diced
- zest and juice of ½ lemon
- 20g flaked almonds, toasted
- salt and pepper

To make the sauce, heat the oil in a large saucepan, add the onion and fry for 3–4 minutes. Add the tomatoes and sugar and season to taste. Cover and simmer for 5 minutes.

Remove the lid and add the herbs and vegetable stock. Simmer for 5 minutes.

Place the couscous in a small saucepan and add about 200ml of the sauce along with the boiling water and cinnamon. Cover and simmer for 5 minutes.

Meanwhile, submerge the cod fillets in the remaining sauce, adding a little hot water if needed. Cover and simmer for 12–15 minutes until the fish is cooked through.

Remove the couscous from the heat and leave to stand for 10 minutes. Fluff up with a fork and add the olives and lemon zest and juice.

Divide the couscous between two dishes, top with the fish and sauce and sprinkle with flaked almonds.

Pan-Fried Salmon Tikka with Jewelled Rice

Using curry paste and natural yogurt is a simple way to spice up your salmon. If you're not a fish fan, simply swap the salmon for chicken breasts or paneer cheese (a traditional Indian cheese) and adjust the cooking time accordingly. Jewelled Rice transforms this midweek meal into something a bit more special, but if you're short on time simply serve it with plain basmati rice or you can get some deliciously spiced microwave rice pouches in the supermarket. (You only need half a portion of Jewelled Rice for this meal but I always cook up the whole amount and keep the rest for lunch the next day.) This dish also goes well with roasted vegetables or a big side salad.

Serves 2

- ½ portion of Jewelled Rice (page 172)
- 2 tbsp tikka paste
- 2 tbsp natural yogurt
- 2 salmon fillets (about 125g each), cut into 3 pieces
- 1 tbsp olive oil
- juice of ½ lemon
- fresh coriander, chopped, to serve
- lemon wedges, to serve

Begin by making the Jewelled Rice (see page 172). While the rice is cooking, prepare the salmon marinade by mixing the tikka pasta with the natural yogurt. Cover each slice of salmon with the marinade.

Heat the oil in a frying pan over a medium heat and add the salmon. Cook for 1–2 minutes on each side.

Divide the Jewelled Rice between two bowls, top with the salmon pieces and squeeze over the lemon juice. Serve garnished with chopped coriander and lemon wedges.

Grilled Prawn and Pepper Skewers

This simple midweek meal pairs lightly spiced prawns with a sweet mango salsa – a colourful, delicious and nutritious meal that requires less than 15 minutes to cook. You'll need eight wooden skewers for this recipe and, if the weather is hot enough to inspire you to have a BBQ, instead of grilling the skewers, you can cook them on the BBQ!

Serves 2

- 200g raw prawns, ready peeled
- 1 yellow pepper, cut into 1 inch squares
- 1 red pepper, cut into 1 inch squares
- ½ red onion, cut into 1cm squares
- 2 tbsp olive oil
- zest and juice of ½ lemon
- ½ tsp chilli flakes
- 25g breadcrumbs (shop-bought or make your own by popping a slice of stale bread into a food processor) or desiccated coconut
- salt and pepper
- green salad, to serve

Preheat the grill to high, line a baking tray with foil and soak the skewers in cold water for 5–10 minutes to prevent them from burning.

Thread the prawns, peppers and onion onto the skewers, alternating between the prawns and the vegetables.

Mix the oil, lemon zest and juice and chilli flakes in a bowl and brush over the skewers.

Spread the breadcrumbs or desiccated coconut out on a plate and dip each skewer in the crumbs to lightly coat, then place on the prepared baking tray. Season to taste.

Grill the skewers for about 3 minutes on each side or until the prawns are pink. Serve with a green salad.

Serving suggestion:
Crispy Smashed Potatoes (page 171) or Mango Salsa (page 178).

Sausage and Olive Pizza

Sausages, olives and tomatoes are a traditional combination from Sardinia and the pecorino or Parmesan cheese adds a lovely tang to the earthiness of the sausage. If you don't eat meat then lentils and mushrooms give a similar taste and texture, and if you're vegan then swap the pecorino or Parmesan for nutritional yeast for a similar cheesy finish.

Serves 2

For the base
- 250g plain flour
- 1 tsp baking powder
- 1 tsp salt
- 1 tbsp olive oil
- 150–200ml warm water

For the topping
- ½ x 400g tin chopped tomatoes
- 2 good-quality raw Italian sausages, skins removed and meat crumbled (or mix together 200g puy lentils, 100g chopped mushrooms, 1 crushed garlic clove, 1 tbsp mixed herbs and ½ tsp caster sugar)
- 50g olives, pitted and chopped
- 2 tsp dried oregano
- 50g Parmesan or pecorino cheese

Serve with a handful of rocket scattered on top

Preheat the oven to 220°C and lightly oil a large baking tray.

Combine the flour, baking powder and salt in a bowl and make a well in the centre. Pour in the oil and 150ml of warm water. Mix with a wooden spoon until it forms a dough, adding a little more water if the mixture is too dry or more flour if it seems too wet.

Knead the dough for a couple of minutes and place on the baking tray. Use your fingertips or use a rolling pin to spread the dough out into a rectangle about 1cm thick and brush with a little olive oil.

Spread over the tomatoes, leaving a 1–2cm thick border around the edge of the dough. Top with the crumbled sausage (or lentil mixture), olives, oregano and cheese and bake for 20 minutes or until the base is golden brown. Serve with rocket leaves.

Family Feasts and Fakeaways

This section is all about bringing family and friends together to create memories while enjoying delicious food. These recipes are inspired by some of the nation's favourite takeaway dishes. They are packed full of nutrients and flavour, are simple to make and perfect for pleasing a crowd.

Fish and Chips

Traditional fish and chips is a great British classic and, as I live by the coast in Brighton, I have it pretty often! This recipe is a beautiful balance of tastes, textures and nutrients: the fish is sweet and lemony and packed full of protein; the chips are crispy and perfectly salty and a great source of carbs; and you get a good dose of healthy fat from the olive oil and vitamins from the peas. You can swap classic chips for Spicy Sweet Potato Wedges (page 168) if you fancy something a bit different.

Serves 4

For the chips
- 800g potatoes (I find Maris Piper work best), sliced into 1cm-thick chips
- 2 tbsp olive oil
- ½ tsp salt

For the fish
- 75g breadcrumbs or ground almonds
- zest of 1 lemon
- 25g Parmesan, grated
- ½ tsp salt
- ½ tsp paprika
- 1 tbsp olive oil
- 4 white fish fillets (skinless and boneless), such as cod or haddock (about 150g each)
- 320g peas, to serve (if you want crushed peas just mash the peas with a knob of butter and a squeeze of lemon once they are cooked)

Preheat the oven to 180°C and bring a large pan of salted water to the boil. Add the sliced potatoes and cook for 4–5 minutes. Drain, return to the saucepan and shake the pan a little to rough up the edges – this will make the chips extra crispy. Add the oil and salt to the pan, coat the chips evenly and spread them out in a single layer on a baking tray. Bake in the oven for 30 minutes, giving them a shake about halfway through cooking.

Make the crust for the fish by mixing the breadcrumbs or ground almonds, lemon zest, Parmesan, salt, paprika and olive oil together in a bowl. Place the fish on a baking tray and spoon over the crust. Add to the oven when the chips have 10–12 minutes left to cook and bake until the flesh of the fish is white and the crumbs are golden.

Serve with peas or other roasted vegetables.

Peri-Peri Halloumi and Portobello Mushroom Burgers

Serving these Peri-Peri burgers with lots of sides is a great way to celebrate the weekend. They are easy to make and perfect for a cosy night in so you can have a proper catch up with friends. You can swap the halloumi for chicken breasts or slices of tofu and make the sauce as mild or as hot as you like.

Serves 4

- 4 corn on the cobs
- 4 Portobello mushrooms
- 2 tbsp olive oil
- 1 x 250g block halloumi, sliced into 8
- 4 tbsp Peri-Peri Marinade, homemade (page 179) or shop-bought
- 4 burger buns
- 4 leaves iceberg lettuce or handful of spinach

Serving suggestion:
Green salad, Warm Brussels Sprout Slaw (page 172) and Spicy Sweet Potato Wedges (page 168).

Preheat the grill to medium. Place the corn on the cobs in a large pan. Cover with water, bring to the boil and reduce the heat to a simmer. Cook for 15 minutes or until the corn is tender.

Place the mushrooms on a baking tray. Brush with 1 tablespoon of oil and place under the preheated grill for 6–8 minutes.

While the mushrooms and corn are cooking, coat the halloumi in two tablespoons of the Peri-Peri Marinade. Heat the remaining oil in a small frying pan or griddle pan if you have one and fry the halloumi for 1–2 minutes on each side. (If you're substituting the halloumi with chicken or tofu, see page 75 for cooking instructions.)

To serve, slice the buns in half horizontally, top the base of each with lettuce or spinach, one mushroom, two slices of halloumi and the remaining Peri-Peri Marinade. Place the other half of the bun on top and serve with the sweetcorn and a selection of sides.

Paneer Masala

Masala means 'spice mix' in Hindi and this recipe is packed full of spices for flavour, heat and to help with digestion. This dish is a healthy and nutritious twist on one of the most popular takeaway curries of them all – Chicken Tikka Masala. Curries are a great way to bring friends together to feast and connect so feel free to use the recipe below as a guide and switch the paneer cheese for four chicken breasts, a 400g block of tofu, two 225g blocks of halloumi or two tins of chickpeas to suit the tastes of your guests.

Serves 4

- 2 tbsp olive oil
- 1 onion, diced
- 2 garlic cloves, crushed
- ½ tsp cinnamon
- ½ tsp chilli powder
- 1 tsp garam masala
- 1 tsp paprika
- 1 tsp cumin
- 1 tsp ground coriander
- ½ tsp turmeric
- 2 tbsp tomato puree
- 1 x 400g tin chopped tomatoes
- 2 x 225g blocks paneer, cubed
- 2 tbsp natural yogurt
- 2 tbsp fresh coriander, chopped
- salt and pepper
- 500g cooked rice to serve (200g dried weight or 2 packets of mircrowaveable rice)
- lime wedges, to serve

Make the masala sauce by heating one tablespoon of oil in a large pan. Add the onion and fry for 2–3 minutes before adding the garlic, spices, tomato puree, tinned tomatoes and 200ml of water. Season to taste and bring to the boil. Simmer for 5 minutes.

In a separate pan, heat the remaining oil and fry the paneer for 10 minutes or until golden. Once cooked, add the paneer to the sauce. Simmer for a further 10 minutes or until the sauce has thickened.

Remove from the heat, stir in the yogurt and sprinkle over the coriander. Serve with rice and lime wedges.

Quinoa and Kidney Bean Burgers

These burgers are great for family get-togethers. They're full of protein from the quinoa and kidney beans and hold together without needing an egg, making them a perfect vegan meal. I love them served in a toasted sourdough bun with a big side salad and they are also delicious with Coconut Curried Kale (page 168) and Warm Brussels Sprout Slaw (page 172).

Serves 4

- 100g quinoa (dried weight)
- 2 x 400g tins kidney beans, drained (480g drained weight)
- 1 tsp salt
- juice of 1 lemon
- 1 onion, diced
- 2 garlic cloves, crushed
- 4 tbsp sesame seeds
- 2 tbsp fresh coriander, chopped
- 1–4 tbsp plain flour
- 1 tbsp olive oil

Rinse the quinoa and add to a pan with 300ml of water. Bring to the boil and cook for 25 minutes, adding more water if needed.

Once the quinoa is cooked, drain it and rinse under cold water. Place in a blender along with the kidney beans, salt, lemon juice, onion, garlic, sesame seeds and coriander and blend until the beans are crushed and the rest of the ingredients are combined. You should have a fairly thick mixture that can be shaped into burgers so if the mixture seems too wet, add one tablespoon of flour at a time until it thickens (you haven't done anything wrong – the texture of the mixture varies depending on the brand of beans and quinoa you use!).

Lay out a large sheet of cling film and place one heaped tablespoon (about 110g) of the mixture in the centre. Loosely wrap the cling film around the mixture to prevent your hands from getting sticky and shape into a large patty no more than 1cm thick. Repeat with the remaining mixture until you have 8 patties and leave to cool in the fridge for around 30 minutes to help the burgers keep their shape during cooking.

Heat the oil in a large frying pan and cook the burgers for 4–5 minutes on each side (you may have to fry them in batches).

Serve in a bun with a salad or with your favourite dips, dressings, sauces and sides (see pages 167–179).

Coconut and Aubergine Dhal

Subtly spiced, beautifully creamy and oh-so-comforting, this is the perfect weekend supper for a chilly winter's evening. Aubergines go beautifully with the sweetness of the coconut, but feel free to experiment with other vegetables such as roasted courgette, red pepper and butternut squash. I love to top my dhal with toasted coconut chips and flaked almonds for added crunch.

Serves 4

- 2 large aubergines, cut into 2cm cubes
- 2 tbsp oil
- 4 garlic cloves, crushed
- 2 tsp cumin
- ½ onion, sliced
- 2 tbsp grated fresh ginger
- 1 tsp turmeric
- 1 tbsp curry powder
- 250g dried red lentils
- 1 x 400ml tin coconut milk
- 2 tbsp fresh coriander, chopped
- salt and pepper
- 500g cooked rice, to serve (200g dried weight or 2 packets of mircowave rice)
- Toasted coconut chips or flaked almonds, to serve

Preheat the oven to 180°C. Toss the chopped aubergine with one tablespoon of oil, two crushed garlic cloves and one teaspoon of cumin. Place on a baking tray and roast in the oven for 20–25 minutes.

While the aubergine is roasting, prepare the dhal by heating the rest of the oil in a large saucepan and adding the onion, remaining garlic and cumin, ginger, turmeric and curry powder. Fry for 2–3 minutes and then add the lentils, coconut milk and 250ml of water and bring to the boil. Simmer for 15–20 minutes, adding more water if needed. Season to taste.

Divide the lentil dhal between four bowls, spoon the roasted aubergine on top and sprinkle over the fresh coriander, toasted coconut chips or flaked almonds. Serve with rice.

Burrito Bowl

Burritos and burrito bowls are a popular takeaway dish and perfect for family gatherings as you can play around with lots of toppings and fillings to please everyone. They are easy to make at home and you can pack them full of nutritious ingredients that will leave you feeling great. I love to serve mine with baked tortilla chips (page 124), guacamole and a dollop of sour cream. I often make extra so I can have leftovers in wraps (like a traditional burrito!) for lunch the next day.

Serves 4

- 1 tbsp olive oil
- 2 garlic cloves, crushed
- 1 x 400g tin black beans or kidney beans, drained and rinsed (240g drained weight)
- 1 tsp chilli powder
- 1 tsp cumin
- ½ tsp salt
- 500g cooked brown rice (about 250g dried weight or you can use 2 packs of microwave rice here)
- juice of 1 lime
- 250g cooked chicken, shredded (see page 75 for how to cook moist and tender chicken breasts) or 1 x 400g tin chickpeas, drained (240g drained weight)
- 2 avocados, sliced
- 160g cherry tomatoes, quartered
- 160g sweetcorn, tinned or frozen and thawed

Heat the oil in a large frying pan and add the garlic. Fry for 1–2 minutes and then add in the beans, chilli powder, cumin and salt, along with 200ml of water. Bring to the boil and simmer for 5–7 minutes until the liquid has evaporated.

Reheat the rice either in the microwave or in a pan and stir through the lime juice (see page 74 for more details on how to cook, store and reheat rice).

Divide the rice between four bowls and top with the bean mixture, chicken or chickpeas, avocados, tomatoes and sweetcorn.

Egg-Fried Rice with Prawns

This stir-fry is the perfect budget-friendly family meal to use up leftover rice and vegetables. It's packed with vitamins from the vegetables, has plenty of protein from the eggs and prawns, and only takes about 15 minutes to cook – much quicker than a takeaway and still a delicious dish to share with friends and family!

Serves 4

- 2 tbsp toasted sesame oil
- 2 garlic cloves, crushed
- 1 red chilli, thinly sliced
- 8 spring onions, sliced
- 1 head broccoli, cut into florets
- 500g cooked basmati or long-grain rice (about 200g dried weight or 2 x 250g packets microwave rice)
- 2 eggs, beaten
- 250g cooked prawns, fresh or frozen and defrosted
- 200g frozen peas
- 1 tbsp soy sauce
- 4 lemon wedges, to serve

Heat the oil in a wok and add the garlic, chilli and spring onions. Fry for 1–2 minutes, then add the broccoli florets with four tablespoons of water. Simmer for 3–4 minutes until the broccoli is tender and the water has evaporated. Add the cooked rice, stir and fry for another minute.

Push the rice and vegetables to the side of the wok and add the beaten eggs into the empty side. Let them set a little and then scramble them in with the rest of the ingredients.

Add the prawns and peas, stir and fry for another 2–3 minutes until the peas are defrosted and the prawns are warmed through. Stir through the soy sauce.

Divide between four bowls and serve with lemon wedges.

Jamaican Jerk-Roasted Vegetables with Rice and Beans

'Rice and beans' is a staple in Caribbean cuisine. It tastes delicious and provides you with a great source of protein and carbs. Combining the rice and beans with jerk-spiced vegetables in this recipe gives you a delicious meal packed with nutrients. I love serving mine with Mango Salsa (page 178) for added sweetness.

Serves 4

For the vegetables
- 4–5 tbsp Jamaican Jerk Marinade, homemade (page 179) or shop-bought
- ½ butternut squash, peeled and diced
- 1 green pepper, diced
- 1 red pepper, diced
- 1 aubergine, diced

For the rice
- 200g wholegrain rice (dried weight)
- 200ml tinned coconut milk
- 1 garlic clove, crushed
- ½ tsp dried thyme
- 8 spring onions, chopped
- 2 x 400g tin kidney beans (480g drained weight)

Make the Jamaican Jerk Marinade according to the recipe on page 179 if you're making it yourself. Place the chopped vegetables in a bowl and cover with the marinade. Leave for two hours in the fridge to get a richer flavour.

Preheat the oven to 180°C. Empty the marinated vegetables into a roasting tin and cook for 25–30 minutes or until the squash is tender.

While the vegetables are roasting, prepare the rice by rinsing, placing in a pan with the coconut milk, garlic, thyme and spring onions and adding just enough water to cover. Bring to the boil and simmer for 20 minutes. Stir in the beans and simmer for another 5–10 minutes or until the rice is tender and has absorbed the water and coconut milk.

Spoon the rice and beans into four bowls and serve with the jerk-roasted vegetables on the side.

Sides, Sauces, Dips and Dressings

Sometimes it's all the extras that really make a meal. Here, I've included a selection of meat and vegetable dishes to serve alongside your main meals or to add to your lunches. There are also mouth-watering marinades to make meat, fish and tofu extra-tasty, delicious dressings to tart up your salads and simple sauces to spice up your stir-fries.

Spicy Sweet Potato Wedges

Sweet potatoes are nutritious and so versatile. These wedges go brilliantly with the Peri-Peri Halloumi and Portobello Mushroom Burgers (page 156) and they are delicious cold too – just pop any leftovers in an airtight container for your lunch the next day.

Serves 4

- 4 medium sweet potatoes (about 200g each), sliced into 8 wedges each
- 3 tbsp olive oil
- 1 tbsp dried mixed herbs
- 1 tsp black pepper
- 1½ tsp salt
- 1 tsp chilli flakes
- a pinch of caster sugar

Preheat the oven to 220°C and line a baking tray with foil (shiny side up).

Place the sweet potato wedges in a bowl. Add the olive oil and the remaining ingredients and mix to coat evenly.

Arrange the wedges on the prepared baking tray and bake in the oven for 30 minutes, turning after 15 minutes. Turn the heat up to 240°C and bake for a further 3–5 minutes to make the wedges extra-crispy.

Coconut Curried Kale

There are much tastier ways to eat kale than blending it into a smoothie and this recipe is one of them!

Serves 4

- 1 tbsp olive or coconut oil
- 1 onion, diced
- 3 garlic cloves, crushed
- 300g kale, roughly chopped
- 2 tbsp curry powder
- ½ tsp salt
- 60g desiccated coconut
- 30g raisins

Heat the oil in a large frying pan or wok and add the onions and garlic. Fry for 2–3 minutes, then add the kale, curry powder and salt with two tablespoons of water. Stir-fry for 3–4 minutes until the kale is bright green but not wilted.

Remove from the heat and stir in the desiccated coconut and raisins.

Honey and Sesame Steak Strips

This meaty side dish is oozing with sweet and spicy flavours and is packed full of protein making it a great addition to salads and stir-fries. As a guide, when having meat as a side dish, have around 80–100g meat (raw weight) and then fill your plate with lots of other delicious and nutritious foods that make you feel great.

Serves 4

- 400g minute steak, cut into 1cm strips
- 2 tbsp honey
- 2 tbsp soy sauce
- 1 tsp chilli flakes
- ½ tsp black pepper
- 1 tbsp sesame seeds
- 1 tbsp olive oil

Place the steak strips in a bowl and add the honey, soy sauce, chilli flakes and black pepper. Stir to combine and leave to marinate for 5–10 minutes.

Heat a wok on high heat and add the oil. Tip in the steak strips and marinade and fry for 2 minutes. Add in the sesame seeds and fry for another minute, stirring regularly to make sure the steak is cooked through.

Serve on top of salads, in wraps, instead of tofu in the Rice Noodle Salad (page 128) or with a selection of sides like Jewelled Rice (page 172) and Coconut Curried Kale (page 168).

Tiny Turkey Burgers

Making vegetables the star of the show and serving meat as a side dish is a great way to ensure your meals are packed full of nutrients. But if you enjoy more meat-based meals then these tiny turkey burgers are a great addition to salads and pasta dishes. Make up a batch in advance and keep them in the fridge for 2–3 days to pop on top of your favourite dishes.

**Serves 4
(makes 12 mini burgers)**

- 400g lean turkey mince
- 2 garlic cloves, crushed
- 10 spring onions, finely chopped
- 1 apple, grated
- 2 tsp dried thyme
- 1 egg
- 30g breadcrumbs or almond flour
- salt and pepper
- 1–2 tbsp olive oil

Mix together all the ingredients except for the olive oil in a bowl and season with a little salt and pepper. Shape into 12 mini burgers using your hands.

Heat 1 tablespoon of oil in a large frying pan over medium to high heat and fry the burgers for 3–4 minutes on each side until the meat begins to brown and is cooked through. If you need to cook the burgers in batches instead of all in one go, add a little extra oil to the pan in between.

Crispy Smashed Potatoes

This is one of my favourite sides to add to salads and serve with seafood. Add a squeeze of lemon for a little extra zing.

Serves 4

- 500g new potatoes
- 2 tbsp olive oil
- 2 garlic cloves, crushed
- salt and pepper

Preheat the oven to 200°C and lightly oil a baking tray.

Place the potatoes in a saucepan, cover with water and bring to the boil. Cook for 15–20 minutes until tender, then drain.

Empty the potatoes onto the prepared baking tray and smash with a potato masher or the bottom of a glass jar. Drizzle with the oil and spoon over the crushed garlic. Season to taste and roast for 20 minutes or until golden and crispy.

Sweet Potato Rostis

These are a great alternative to toast and are delicious topped with boiled or poached eggs. I also love serving them instead of a burger bun.

Serves 4 (makes 8 rostis)

- 4 medium sweet potatoes (about 200g each), peeled and grated
- 1 onion, diced
- 2 eggs, beaten
- 1 tbsp olive oil
- salt and pepper

Place the grated sweet potatoes in a bowl with the onion and eggs. Season to taste and mix well.

Divide the mixture into eight and shape into patties, squeezing out any excess liquid.

Heat the oil in a frying pan over a medium heat and cook the patties for 4–5 minutes, flattening them with a fish slice so they are 1–2cm thick. Turn the patties over and cook for another 4–5 minutes until they are crisp and golden.

Jewelled Rice

Spicy, comforting and beautiful to look at, this is my favourite way to eat rice. It's guaranteed to jazz up any meal.

Serves 4

- 200g basmati rice
- 1 tbsp olive oil
- 1 onion, diced
- 1 medium carrot, grated
- ½ tsp turmeric
- ½ tsp cumin
- ½ tsp cinnamon
- 1 tsp salt
- 50g raisins
- seeds of ½ pomegranate (see page 104)
- 50g nuts (such as pistachios or almonds)
- juice of ½ lemon

Soak the rice in cold water for 10–15 minutes, drain and rinse.

Heat the olive oil in a large saucepan and add the onion, carrot, spices and salt. Fry for 2–3 minutes and then add the rice. Stir so the spices coat the grains and add enough water to cover the rice. Bring to the boil and simmer for 10–12 minutes until the rice has absorbed all the water.

Remove from the heat, add the raisins, pomegranate seeds and nuts and squeeze over the lemon juice. Stir to combine.

Warm Brussels Sprout Slaw

Brussels sprouts seem to be one of the most hated vegetables yet they are packed full of nutrients and can be delicious if you cook them properly. This recipe is cheap and easy to make and will (hopefully!) transform you into a sprout lover!

Serves 4

- 3 tbsp olive oil
- 1 onion, finely sliced
- 500g Brussels sprouts, trimmed and thinly sliced
- 2 tbsp apple cider vinegar
- 1 tsp wholegrain mustard
- 1 tbsp honey
- juice of ½ lemon
- 50g almonds (with skin), chopped

Heat one tablespoon of oil in a large frying pan and add the onion. Fry for 1–2 minutes. Add the Brussels sprouts and fry for another 3–4 minutes until tender.

Combine the rest of the oil with the apple cider vinegar, mustard, honey and lemon juice in a small jar and shake to mix. Add to the frying pan along with the almonds and fry for a further 1–2 minutes. Serve warm.

Roasted Cauliflower with Mushrooms, Raisins and Walnuts

This is delicious paired with anything cheesy and is perfect with pasta dishes. Any leftovers can be eaten for lunch the next day too!

Serves 4

- 1 head cauliflower, cut into bite-sized florets
- 150g mushrooms, quartered
- 2 tbsp olive oil
- 1 tsp dried oregano or thyme
- 1 tsp chilli flakes
- ½ tsp salt
- 40g raisins
- 30g walnuts, chopped
- juice of ½ lemon

Preheat the oven to 180°C and bring a large pan of water to the boil. Add the cauliflower and simmer for 2–3 minutes. Drain and place the cauliflower on a baking tray. You can also lightly steam the cauliflower for 2–3 minutes instead of boiling. Add the mushrooms, drizzle with oil and sprinkle over the herbs and chilli flakes. Season with salt and toss to coat.

Roast in the oven for 20–30 minutes until the cauliflower is starting to turn golden.

Meanwhile, soak the raisins in a small cup of boiling water for 5 minutes to soften and then drain.

Once the cauliflower is cooked, empty it onto a serving plate, scatter over the raisins and walnuts and squeeze over the lemon juice.

Three-Bean Ratatouille

This side goes well with most meat and fish dishes as well as being a delicious and filling main packed full of flavour and fibre. Serve it alongside rice or bread for a simple lunch or dinner or top with a couple of poached eggs for a nutritious breakfast.

Serves 4 as a side or 2 as a main

- 2 tbsp olive oil
- 1 red onion, diced
- 2 garlic cloves, crushed
- ½ red pepper, diced
- ½ yellow pepper, diced
- 1 courgette, cut into 1cm cubes
- 1 small aubergine, cut into 1cm cubes
- 1 tsp chilli flakes
- 1 x 400g tin chopped tomatoes
- 200ml hot water or vegetable stock
- ½ x 400g tin cannellini beans (120g drained weight)
- ½ x 400g tin borlotti beans (120g drained weight)
- 100g green beans
- 1 tbsp dried basil
- zest and juice of ½ lemon
- salt and pepper

Heat the oil in a frying pan and add the onion and garlic. Fry for 3–4 minutes, then add the vegetables and chilli flakes. Fry for 8 minutes, stirring occasionally.

Add the tomatoes and hot water or stock and simmer for 5 minutes.

Add the beans and basil and simmer for another 10 minutes.

Add the lemon zest and juice and season to taste before serving.

Malloreddus (Sardinian Pasta Shells)

I always thought pasta was far too time-consuming and complicated to make until I went to Sardinia and made malloreddus (also known as 'gnocchetti' or 'little gnocchi') with 82-year-old Auntie Annarita in a little village called Mamoiada. This pasta needs nothing more than flour, eggs, salt and water (and a bit of elbow grease to knead the dough!). You can make up a big batch, freeze it and use it for dishes such as the Eight-Ingredient Mediterranean Pasta Salad (page 130) or Super-Green Pasta (page 143). To make a vegan version, just miss out the egg and add more water.

Serves 4

- 500g semolina flour or 00 grade pasta flour
- ½ tsp salt
- 1 egg

Empty the flour into a bowl and mix in the salt. Make a well in the centre and crack in the egg. Mix in, using your hands or the end of a wooden spoon.

Pour in 250ml of water a little at a time and mix until you have a smooth dough. Add more flour if the mixture gets too sticky.

Turn out onto a floured surface and knead for 5–10 minutes until the dough is soft and pliable.

Divide the dough into 12 pieces and roll out with the palms of your hands to form long ropes no more than 1cm thick. Cut or tear off chickpea-sized pieces of the dough.

Either use your thumb to form shells by pressing each little ball of dough into a floured surface and swiping across with a fork, or push each dough ball into the side of a fine sieve or tea strainer to make indented shells.

When ready to cook, bring a large pan of salted water to the boil and add the pasta shells. Cook for 3–4 minutes or until the shells rise to the surface and are al dente (still with a bit of a bite to them).

Lemon and Almond Green Beans

Lemon and almonds are a classic flavour combination that make green beans taste delicious.
You can also try this recipe with broccoli, peas or kale.

Serves 4

- 500g green beans, fresh (trimmed) or frozen and defrosted
- 40g butter
- juice of ½ lemon
- 25g toasted flaked almonds
- ½ tsp salt

Bring a pan of water to the boil. Add the green beans and simmer for 5–6 minutes until tender. Drain and empty into a serving dish.

Melt the butter in a small saucepan and add the lemon juice, almonds and salt. Pour over the green beans.

Roasted Courgette Coins

These courgette 'coins' are a tasty way to get more vegetables into your meals and require barely any preparation. You can add extra vegetables, like peppers, aubergines and mushrooms, to make a big batch of roasted vegetables which will go well with many of the recipes in this book.

Serves 4

- 2 courgettes, thickly sliced
- 2 tbsp olive oil
- ½ tsp salt
- 1 tsp chilli flakes
- juice of ½ lemon

Preheat the oven to 160°C and arrange the sliced courgettes on a baking tray.

Sprinkle over the oil, salt and chilli flakes, squeeze over the lemon juice and roast in the oven for 20–25 minutes until crisp and golden.

Dressings

Dressings can transform a simple salad into something magnificent. Just pop all the ingredients in a jar, shake it up and store in the fridge for up to a week for when you need it. I usually make up a couple of dressings at the weekend to have on hand to drizzle over salads and vegetables when I'm in a rush.

SOY AND GINGER DRESSING

- 2 tbsp toasted sesame oil
- 2 tbsp olive oil
- 2 tbsp soy sauce
- 100ml rice vinegar
- 2 tsp grated fresh ginger
- 1 tsp honey

YOGURT AND MUSTARD DRESSING

- 3 tbsp natural yogurt (about 60g)
- juice of ¼ lemon
- 1 tsp mustard
- ½ tsp salt
- ½ tsp pepper
- warm water – enough to thin

LEMON AND TAHINI DRESSING

- 1 tbsp olive oil
- 3 tbsp tahini
- zest and juice of ½ lemon
- 1 garlic clove, crushed
- ½ tsp salt
- warm water – enough to thin

LEMON AND HERB VINAIGRETTE

- 3 tbsp olive oil
- 1 tsp red wine vinegar
- 1 tsp Dijon mustard
- zest and juice of ½ lemon
- 1 tsp honey
- 1 tsp dried oregano
- 1 tsp dried basil

Salsas

Salsas bring a little bit of summery sweetness to any dish and go really well with prawns and anything spicy. Just combine the ingredients and store in an airtight container in the fridge for 2–3 days so you can add a spoonful to brighten up any meal.

MANGO SALSA

- 2 medium mangoes (about 400g), diced
- 1 red chilli, finely diced
- ½ red onion, finely diced
- 1 medium tomato, chopped
- juice of 1 lime
- ½ tsp salt
- 2 tbsp fresh coriander, chopped

SPICY SALSA

- 400g tomatoes, chopped
- ½ onion, finely diced
- 2 garlic cloves, crushed
- 1 red chilli, finely diced
- juice of ½ lemon
- 2 tbsp fresh coriander, chopped
- ½ tsp salt

Stir-Fry Sauces

Use these sauces in a stir-fry to make a quick and tasty meal in minutes. Just pop the ingredients in a jug, stir well and add to your stir-fry towards the end of cooking for about 4–5 minutes.

BASIC SAUCE
- 3 garlic cloves, crushed
- 3 tbsp soy sauce
- 1 tbsp rice vinegar
- 120ml cold water or vegetable stock
- 1½ tbsp cornflour or arrowroot powder

ORANGE AND GINGER SAUCE
- 3 tbsp soy sauce
- 1 tbsp grated fresh ginger
- 1 tbsp rice vinegar
- 120ml orange juice
- 1½ tbsp cornflour or arrowroot powder

CURRY SAUCE
- 1½ tbsp curry paste
- 1 tbsp brown sugar
- 120ml cold water or vegetable stock
- 1½ tbsp cornflour or arrowroot powder

SWEET CHILLI SAUCE
- 1 tbsp soy sauce
- 2 tbsp tomato puree
- 1 tbsp rice vinegar
- 2 tbsp brown sugar
- 1 tsp dried chilli flakes
- 120ml cold water
- 1½ tbsp cornflour or arrowroot powder

Marinades

These marinades work well with meat, fish, tofu and halloumi as well as vegetables. They are simple to make – just combine the ingredients and mix in a blender to make a smooth paste. When you're ready to use them, smother them over your ingredients – ideally a couple of hours in advance of cooking to get the most flavour out of them.

JAMAICAN JERK MARINADE
- 8 spring onions, sliced
- 1 tbsp grated fresh ginger
- 2 garlic cloves, crushed
- 2 Scotch bonnet chillies, sliced
- ½ tsp thyme
- ¼ tsp cinnamon
- 1 tbsp allspice
- ½ onion, diced
- juice of 1 lime
- 2 tbsp honey
- 2 tbsp soy sauce
- 2 tbsp olive oil

PERI-PERI MARINADE
- 6 red chillies, diced
- 2 garlic cloves, crushed
- 2 tsp salt
- 1 tsp caster sugar
- 1 tsp oregano
- 1 tsp paprika
- 3 tbsp olive oil
- juice of 1 lemon
- 1 roasted red pepper, diced
- 1 roasted onion, diced
- 2 tbsp red wine vinegar

Cakes, Bakes and Sweet Things

There is something very therapeutic about baking and transforming simple ingredients into a delicious and nourishing treat. From bread to cheesecake, these recipes are fun to make and perfect for sharing with guests.

Seedy Soda Bread

If you're new to bread baking, then this recipe is a great one to try because you just chuck everything in a bowl and pop it in the oven – no kneading or waiting for the dough to rise. If you have digestive issues with some breads, then soda bread is good to experiment with because it doesn't contain yeast (which some people find makes them feel bloated). Play around with different flours and try adding in raisins and dried apricots to make a fruity loaf.

Makes 1 small loaf

- 250g spelt flour (wholemeal and rye flour also work well)
- ½ tsp salt
- 1½ tsp bicarbonate of soda
- 40g mixed seeds, plus 1 tbsp for topping
- 200ml buttermilk (if you don't have buttermilk, simply mix 200ml milk with 1 tablespoon of lemon juice and leave to thicken for 5 minutes)

Preheat the oven to 200°C and line a baking tray with baking paper.

In a large bowl, sift the flour, salt and bicarbonate of soda. Add the seeds and mix.

Pour the buttermilk or milk mixture in and mix to form a sticky dough. Empty the dough onto a floured surface and shape into a round loaf.

Place on the prepared baking tray, top with the seeds, dust with flour and cut a deep cross in the top of the dough. Bake for 30 minutes until the bread is golden.

Honey Oat Banana Bread

Hearty, wholesome, moist and not too sweet, this banana bread is perfect as a quick breakfast with a dollop of yogurt, elevenses with a cup of coffee, afternoon tea with a smothering of almond butter or dessert with a drizzle of melted chocolate.

Makes 1 loaf

- 200g oat flour (put oats in a blender until they become a fine powder)
- 100g all-purpose flour
- 2 tsp baking powder
- ½ tsp cinnamon
- ½ tsp salt
- 100ml milk
- 3 tbsp honey
- 3 medium bananas, mashed
- 2 eggs, beaten
- 2 tbsp olive oil
- 1 tsp vanilla extract
- 1 tbsp brown sugar

Preheat the oven to 180°C and grease or line a 900g (2lb) loaf tin.

Mix together the flours, baking powder, cinnamon and salt in a large bowl. In a separate bowl, mix together the milk, honey, mashed banana, eggs, oil and vanilla extract. Once mixed, add the wet ingredients into the dry ingredients.

Mix until smooth and pour the batter into the prepared loaf tin. Sprinkle the brown sugar on top and bake for 40–45 minutes until the bread is risen, golden and cooked through. Leave in the tin for five minutes and then tip out on to a wire rack and leave to cool.

Baklava Cheesecake

This cheesecake combines the nutty flavours of baklava, a traditional Middle Eastern dessert, with the creaminess of a baked cheesecake. It's ideal for dinner parties served with fresh berries. This recipe uses lower-fat cream cheese for a lighter texture, but feel free to use full-fat varieties for a richer, creamier cheesecake.

Makes 10–12 slices

For the syrup
- 10g butter
- 75g mixed nuts, chopped
- 1 tsp cinnamon
- 25g caster sugar
- 1–2 tbsp honey

For the base
- 250g filo pastry (10–12 sheets)
- 10g butter, melted

For the filling
- 2 x 250g tubs light cream cheese
- 150g natural or Greek yogurt
- 3 eggs, beaten
- 150g caster sugar
- 1 tsp vanilla extract

Preheat the oven to 160°C and line a 20–24cm cake tin with baking paper.

Prepare the syrup by heating the butter in a small pan and adding the nuts. Fry for 2–3 minutes before adding the cinnamon, sugar, honey and 40ml of water. Bring to the boil and simmer for 15 minutes without stirring.

While the syrup is cooking, make the base by brushing each sheet of filo pastry with butter before draping in the cake tin. Repeat so the whole tin is covered, allowing the pastry to overhang.

Make the filling by combining all the ingredients in a bowl and mixing until smooth.

Pour the filling into the pastry-lined cake tin and spoon the nutty syrup over, letting some spoonfuls sink to the bottom. Bake for 50–60 minutes until the cheesecake is set, but still has a slight wobble, and leave to cool in the oven with the door open, to avoid it cracking.

Socca (Chickpea Flatbread)

Socca is a traditional Italian flatbread, also known as 'farinata'. It is a great gluten-free alternative to wraps and pizza bases and even though I eat gluten, I often eat soccas because they are so easy to make and have a deliciously nutty taste that goes really well with sweet and spicy toppings and fillings.

Makes 6 flatbreads

- 200g chickpea flour (also known as gram flour)
- ½ tsp salt
- 1 tbsp dried mixed herbs
- ½ tsp cumin
- 2 tbsp olive oil

Preheat the oven to 200°C and line a baking tray with baking paper.

Mix the chickpea flour, salt, herbs, cumin and one tablespoon of olive oil in a bowl and pour in 400ml of water. Whisk to create a smooth batter and leave to rest for at least 30 minutes to allow the chickpea flour to absorb the liquid.

Heat the remaining oil in a medium-sized frying pan over a medium heat and pour in a sixth of the batter. Cook for 2–3 minutes on each side. Repeat with the remaining batter.

Mango and Coconut Dessert

Mango reminds me of my time in Thailand so this dessert brings back lots of happy memories. It only takes around five minutes to make and you can use a selection of your favourite fruit – bananas and berries work beautifully too.

Serves 4

- 50g dark chocolate (75–85 per cent cocoa)
- 15g coconut oil
- 1 x 400ml tin coconut milk, kept in the fridge overnight (to allow the cream to rise)
- ½ tsp vanilla extract
- 2 mangoes, peeled and sliced
- 20g flaked almonds

Place the chocolate and coconut oil in a heatproof bowl and microwave on low for 1–2 minutes, stirring every 15 seconds, until melted.

Drain the coconut water from the tin of coconut milk and place in a bowl. Add the vanilla extract and whisk for 2–3 minutes until stiff peaks form.

Divide the mango slices between four plates, spoon over the coconut cream, drizzle over the chocolate and sprinkle with flaked almonds.

Sweet Potato and Cinnamon Wagashi

The Japanese island Okinawa has become famous for its nutrient-dense purple potatoes which are thought to contribute to the health and longevity of its population. Wagashi are a traditional Okinawan dessert made from purple potatoes or sweet potatoes and are a cross between a cake and a cookie – perfect with an afternoon cuppa!

Makes 8–10

- 2 medium sweet potatoes (about 400g in total)
- 40g coconut flour
- 10g butter or coconut oil, melted
- 20g brown sugar
- ½ tsp cinnamon
- 25g chocolate chips, dark or milk (optional)
- 1 egg yolk, beaten (use melted coconut oil for a vegan alternative)
- 3 tbsp sesame seeds

Preheat the oven to 180°C and line a baking tray with baking paper.

Prick the sweet potatoes with a fork and microwave on high for 8–12 minutes until tender. Leave to cool and scoop out the flesh into a bowl.

Mix the sweet potato flesh with the coconut flour, butter or coconut oil, sugar and cinnamon. Add in the chocolate chips, if using, and then roll the mixture into 8–10 small balls.

Place the balls on the prepared baking tray, brush with egg, sprinkle with sesame seeds and bake for 15–20 minutes until slightly brown.

Almond and Lemon Olive Oil Cake

This is a simple, sumptuous, sunshiney cake full of delicious Mediterranean flavours. It freezes really well too so you can always slice it and pop half in the freezer for when you fancy something sweet and lemony.

Makes 10–12 slices

- 200g caster sugar
- 3 eggs
- zest and juice of 1 lemon
- 175ml olive oil
- 200g plain flour
- 2 tsp baking powder
- ½ tsp salt
- 60ml milk
- 100g toasted flaked almonds

Preheat the oven to 180°C and line a 20cm cake tin with baking paper.

Beat the sugar, eggs and lemon zest and juice in a bowl until pale and fluffy and then beat in the oil.

Add in the flour, baking powder, salt and milk and mix until smooth. Stir through the flaked almonds and empty into the prepared cake tin.

Bake for 35–45 minutes until a knife or skewer inserted into the cake comes out clean. Leave to cool in the tin for 15 minutes before turning out.

Chocolate Berry Bean Cake

Using beans in cake recipes may seem weird but beans have been used in Chinese and Japanese baking for centuries to make cakes richer, denser and moister. They also add protein and give the cake a lovely earthiness which works beautifully with the chocolate and berries in this recipe. Feel free to drizzle the cake with chocolate after baking to make it look extra special.

Makes 8–10 slices

- 1 x 400g tin kidney beans, drained (240g drained weight)
- 75g butter or coconut oil, melted
- 100g plain flour
- 50g cocoa powder
- 1½ tsp baking powder
- 120g light brown sugar
- 3 eggs, beaten
- 1 tsp vanilla extract
- 100g berries (raspberries work beautifully!), fresh or frozen
- few squares of white chocolate, melted, to serve.

Preheat the oven to 180°C and line a 20cm cake tin with baking paper.

Place the kidney beans in a blender and blend to a paste. Add to a bowl with the rest of the ingredients, except the berries, and mix to form a smooth batter.

Stir through the berries, empty into the prepared tin and bake in the oven for 20–25 minutes. Leave to cool in the tin for 10 minutes before turning out.

Chocolate Falafel

These tasty treats are a combination of two of my favourite foods – chocolate and chickpeas! You won't find them on the shelves of supermarkets or in any other cookbooks but they might just be my favourite recipe in the whole book and they proved a firm favourite at my recipe testing parties! If you like a slightly cakier falafel, add in the peanut butter, but if you prefer your falafel to be a little crumblier then leave it out. You can also add nuts, raisins and desiccated coconut for extra flavour and texture.

Makes 10–12 falafel

- 1 x 400g tin chickpeas, drained (240g drained weight)
- ½ tsp baking powder
- 3 tbsp maple syrup or honey
- 30g cocoa powder
- ½ tsp vanilla extract
- 40g peanut butter, crunchy or smooth (optional)
- 40g chocolate chips, dark or milk

Preheat the oven to 160°C and line a baking tray with baking paper.

Place all the ingredients in a blender, except the chocolate chips, and blend until crumbly.

Stir through the chocolate chips and shape the mixture into balls weighing about 30g each. If the mixture seems too wet, then add a little extra cocoa powder. Dampen your hands before shaping to stop the dough sticking to them.

Place the falafel on the prepared baking tray and bake in the oven for 10–15 minutes. The longer you bake them for, the crispier and crumblier they'll be.

Carrot Cake Cookies

Chewy, cakey, cinnamon-y, perfectly sweet, with a little walnut-y crunch, these cookies will not disappoint. You can top them with cream cheese frosting to make them a little more indulgent or crumble over ice cream to make a delicious sundae.

Makes 10–12

- 100g oats
- 100g plain flour
- 1½ tsp baking powder
- 1 tsp cinnamon
- ¼ tsp salt
- 30g butter or coconut oil, melted
- 1 egg, beaten
- 1 tsp vanilla extract
- 5 tbsp maple syrup
- 75g carrot, grated
- 25g walnuts, chopped
- 25g raisins

Combine oats, flour, baking powder, cinnamon and salt in a bowl and set to one side. In a separate bowl mix the butter or coconut oil, egg, vanilla extract and maple syrup.

Add the wet ingredients to the dry and then stir through the carrot, walnuts and raisins. Cover and leave in the fridge for at least 30 minutes so the dough holds its shape better when cooking.

Preheat the oven to 180°C and line a baking tray with baking paper.

Scoop tablespoons of the mixture onto the prepared tray, allowing a little room for the mixture to spread as it cooks, and bake in the oven for 12–15 minutes. Once cooked, transfer to a wire rack to cool. The cookies will harden a little as they cool so make sure you don't overbake them. Keep in a tin in a cool, dry place.

Mug Cakes

These are perfect single serving treats for when you fancy something sweet and don't have much time. Either eat them straight from the mug or turn them out and serve with yogurt, ice cream or custard. Mug cakes are a fun way to play around with flavours and try new recipes so use the ideas below as a guide and add in your favourite ingredients. I'd recommend using a large mug to give the cakes room to rise and avoid any mug cake explosions! (Also, please ensure you use microwave-proof mugs.)

RASPBERRY AND FRANGIPANE MUG CAKE

- 15g butter or coconut oil
- 20g caster sugar
- 20g plain flour
- 20g ground almonds
- ½ tsp baking powder
- 1 egg, beaten
- 20ml milk
- 6 raspberries

Place the butter or coconut oil in a mug and warm in the microwave on medium for 20 seconds.

Mix in all the other ingredients, except the raspberries, and then pop the raspberries on top.

Microwave on high for 1½–2 minutes or until risen and spongy.

CHOCOLATE CHIP MUG CAKE

- 15g butter or coconut oil
- 20g caster sugar
- 45g plain flour
- ½ tsp baking powder
- 1 egg, beaten
- 40ml milk
- ½ tsp vanilla extract
- 10g chocolate chips

Place the butter or coconut oil in a mug and warm in the microwave on medium for 20 seconds.

Mix in all the other ingredients and microwave on high for 1½–2 minutes or until risen and spongy.

Final Words

My hope is that by the time you get to these final words, you will feel like someone slightly different to the person you were when you first started reading this book.

My hope is that you will have learned about yourself and your relationship with food and you are beginning to enjoy the health and happiness that comes from truly nourishing your body.

My hope is that you will have let go of the fear and guilt, the rules and restrictions, and the self-deprivation and self-doubt.

My hope is that you are using your struggles with food as an opportunity to learn how to live with less fear and more freedom.

I would love to hear about your fear-free journey so please get in touch via my website at www.FearFreeFood.co.uk or you can find me on social media: @NicolaJaneHobbs.

Happy eating!

Nicola x

Acknowledgements

Fear-Free Food is an idea that I have been brewing for years. After finding freedom from my own struggles with food, I wanted to funnel my experience into something meaningful. But for years I was scared to share my message because my approach to healthy eating is different to the norm of dieting and deprivation. So I would like to acknowledge all those who helped me find my voice, encouraged me to speak out and have given me the opportunity to share my fear-free message with the world.

The support I've had in writing this book has been absolutely breathtaking so I would like to thank everyone who has been involved in its creation. There are far too many people to name individually, but you know who you are. To everyone who has shared their knowledge, read my drafts, helped me refine my ideas, inspired me with their research, checked my commas are in the right places, tested the recipes, helped me clean up my kitchen after multiple messy cooking experiments, and reassured me that my message matters – thank you. And, of course, to my editors and publishers – thank you for giving me the opportunity to write *Fear-Free Food* and for transforming my vision into such a beautiful book.

I would also like to thank all those who supported me to find freedom from my own food struggles all those years ago. The love you gave me helped me to find freedom and I have channelled that love into *Fear-Free Food* so others can join me in eating freely, loving fiercely and living fearlessly.

Helpful Contacts

To contact me, find more recipe inspiration and get further support with eating, see
www.FearFreeFood.co.uk

You can also get in touch on social media:
Instagram: @NicolaJaneHobbs
Twitter: @NicolaJaneHobbs
Facebook Page: Nicola Jane Hobbs

Use the hashtag **#FearFreeFood** to share your recipe creations.

If you need further advice and support, please see the contacts below:

Beat
The UK's leading eating disorder charity.
www.b-eat.co.uk

National Eating Disorder Association
The leading non-profit organisation in the US for individuals and families affected by eating disorders.
www.nationaleatingdisorders.org

British Dietetic Association
Provides a list of Registered Dieticians in the UK.
www.bda.uk.com

The Academy of Nutrition and Dietetics
Provides a list of Registered Dietitian Nutritionists in the USA.
www.eatright.org/find-an-expert

Intuitive Eating
Provides a list of Certified Intuitive Eating Counselors worldwide.
www.intuitiveeating.org/certified-counselors

Conversion Chart for Common Measurements

US	Metric
1 teaspoon	5 mililitres
1 tablespoon (3 teaspoons)	15 mililitres
1 fluid ounce (2 tablespoons)	30 mililitres
¼ cup	60 mililitres
⅓ cup	80 mililitres
½ cup	120 mililitres
1 cup	240 mililitres
1 pint (2 cups)	480 mililitres
1 quart (4 cups; 32 ounces)	960 mililitres
1 gallon (4 quarts)	3.84 litres
1 ounce (by weight)	28 grams
1 pound	454 grams
2.2 pounds	1 kilogram

°F	°C	Gas Mark
250	120	½
275	140	1
300	150	2
325	160	3
350	170	4
375	190	5
400	200	6
425	220	7
450	230	8
475	240	9
500	260	10

SOURCES

Page 10: Press Association (2013, January 20). 'Women own up to guilt over eating habits'. *Guardian*. Retrieved from www.theguardian.com.

Page 10: Steenhuis, I. (2009). 'Guilty or not? Feelings of guilt about food among college women'. *Appetite*, 52(2), 531–534.

Page 10: Wang, Y. C., McPherson, K., Marsh, T., Gortmaker, S. L. & Brown, M. (2011). 'Health and economic burden of the projected obesity trends in the USA and the UK'. *The Lancet*, 378(9793), 815–825.

Page 10: Caleyachetty, R., Thomas, G. N., Toulis, K. A., Mohammed, N., Gokhale, K. M., Balachandran, K. & Nirantharakumar, K. (2017). 'Metabolically healthy obese and incident cardiovascular disease events among 3.5 million men and women'. *Journal of the American College of Cardiology*, 70(12), 1429–1437.

Page 10: McManus, S., Meltzer, H., Brugha, T. & Bebbington, P., *Adult Psychiatric Morbidity in England, 2007: Results of a Household Survey*, The NHS Information Centre.

Page 10: Hudson, J. I., Hiripi, E., Pope, H. G. & Kessler, R. C. (2007). 'The prevalence and correlates of eating disorders in the National Comorbidity Survey Replication'. *Biological Psychiatry*, 61(3), 348–358.

Page 17: Dulloo, A. G., Jacquet, J. & Montani, J. P. (2012). 'How dieting makes some fatter: From a perspective of human body composition autoregulation'. *Proceedings of the Nutrition Society*, 71(3), 379–389.

Page 17: de Witt Huberts, J. C., Evers, C. & de Ridder, D. T. (2013). 'Double trouble: Restrained eaters do not eat less and feel worse'. *Psychology & Health*, 28(6), 686–700.

Page 17: Schaefer, J. T. & Magnuson, A. B. (2014). 'A review of interventions that promote eating by internal cues'. *Journal of the Academy of Nutrition and Dietetics*, 114(5), 734–760.

Page 17: Bacon, L., Keim, N. L., Van Loan, M. D., Derricote, M., Gale, B., Kazaks, A. & Stern, J. S. (2002). 'Evaluating a "non-diet" wellness intervention for improvement of metabolic fitness, psychological well-being and eating and activity behaviors'. *International Journal of Obesity*, 26(6), 854.

Page 22: Buettner, D. (2012). *The Blue Zones: 9 lessons for living longer from the people who've lived the longest*. National Geographic Books.

Page 23: Yates, L. & Warde, A. (2017). 'Eating together and eating alone: Meal arrangements in British households'. *The British Journal of Sociology*, 68(1), 97–118.

Page 23: The NPD Group (2014, August 6). 'Consumers are alone over half of eating occasions as a result of changing lifestyles and more single-person households'. Retrieved from www.npd.com.

Page 23: The Nutrition Source, Department of Nutrition, Harvard School of Public Health (2011). 'The Problems with the Food Guide Pyramid and MyPyramid'. Retrieved from www.hsph.harvard.edu/nutritionsource.

Page 25: Scrinis, G. (2002). 'Sorry, Marge'. *Meanjin*, 61(4), 108–116.

Page 25: Dodds, A. & Chamberlain, K. (2017). The problematic messages of nutritional discourse: A case-based critical media analysis'. *Appetite*, 108, 42–50.

Page 25: Lauroly (2013, January 28). 'The art of savoring… the "Master of Taste", Dr. Paul Rozin Checks in from Paris'. Retrieved from www.worldwisebeauty.com.

Page 25: Tribole, E. & Resch, E. (2012). *Intuitive Eating*, New York: Macmillan, 132–148.

Page 26: Rozin, P., Kabnick, K., Pete, E., Fischler, C. & Shields, C. (2003). 'The ecology of eating smaller portion sizes in France than in the United States help explain the French paradox'. *Psychological Science*, 14(5), 450–454.

Page 26: Rozin, P., Remick, A. K., & Fischler, C. (2011). 'Broad themes of difference between French and Americans in attitudes to food and other life domains: Personal versus communal values, quantity versus quality, and comforts versus joys'. *Frontiers in Psychology*, 2, 177.

Page 26: Koritar, P., Philippi, S. T. & dos Santos Alvarenga, M. (2017). 'Attitudes toward health and taste of food among women with bulimia nervosa and women of a non-clinical sample'. *Appetite*, 113, 172–177.

Page 26: Papies, E., Stroebe, W. & Aarts, H. (2007). 'Pleasure in the mind: Restrained eating and spontaneous hedonic thoughts about food'. *Journal of Experimental Social Psychology*, 43(5), 810–817.

Page 27: Trofholz, A. C., Tate, A. D., Miner, M. H. & Berge, J. M. (2017). 'Associations between TV viewing at family meals and the emotional atmosphere of the meal, meal healthfulness, child dietary intake, and child weight status'. *Appetite*, 108, 361–366.

Page 27: Berge, J. M., Wall, M., Hsueh, T. F., Fulkerson, J. A., Larson, N. & Neumark-Sztainer, D. (2015). 'The protective role of family meals for youth obesity: 10-year longitudinal associations'. *The Journal of Pediatrics*, 166(2), 296–301.

Page 27: Capaldi, C. A., Dopko, R. L. & Zelenski, J. M. (2014). 'The relationship between nature connectedness and happiness: A meta-analysis'. *Frontiers in Psychology*, 5, 976.

Page 28: Schaefer, J. T. & Magnuson, A. B. (2014). 'A review of interventions that promote eating by internal cues'. *Journal of the Academy of Nutrition and Dietetics*, 114(5), 734–760.

Page 28: Ackard, D. M., Croll, J. K. & Kearney-Cooke, A. (2002). 'Dieting frequency among college females: Association with disordered eating, body image, and related psychological problems'. *Journal of Psychosomatic Research*, 52(3), 129–136.

Page 28: Clifford, D., Ozier, A., Bundros, J., Moore, J., Kreiser, A. & Morris, M. N. (2015). 'Impact of non-diet approaches on attitudes, behaviours, and health outcomes: A systematic review'. *Journal of Nutrition Education and Behaviour*, 47(2), 143–155.

Page 28: Fiske, L., Fallon, E. A., Blissmer, B. & Redding, C. A. (2014). 'Prevalence of body dissatisfaction among United States adults: Review and recommendations for future research'. *Eating Behaviors*, 15(3), 357–365.

Page 28: Tribole, E. (2017) 'Intuitive Eating: Research Update'. *Sports, Cardiovascular, and Wellness Nutrition Pulse*, 36(3), 1–5.

Page 29: De Souza, R. J., Mente, A., Maroleanu, A., Cozma, A. I., Ha, V., Kishibe, T. & Anand, S. S. (2015). 'Intake of saturated and trans unsaturated fatty acids and risk of all cause mortality, cardiovascular disease, and type 2 diabetes: Systematic review and meta-analysis of observational studies'. *BMJ*, 351, h3978.

Page 29: US Department of Health and Human Services (2016). US Department of Agriculture. *Dietary Guidelines for Americans 2015–2020*. Retrieved from www.health.gov.

Page 30: Hauff, C. (2016). 'Hashtagging your health: Using psychosocial variables and social media use to understand impression management and exercise behavior in women'. Doctoral dissertation: The University of Wisconsin-Milwaukee.

Page 30: O'Brien, K. (2015). 'The Cultivation of Eating Disorders Through Instagram (master's thesis)'. Retrieved from Scholar Commons. http://scholarcommons.usf.edu/etd/6004.

Page 30: Holland, G. & Tiggemann, M. (2016). 'A systematic review of the impact of the use of social networking sites on body image and disordered eating outcomes'. *Body Image*, 17, 100–110.

Page 30: Turner, P. G. & Lefevre, C. E. (2017). 'Instagram use is linked to increased symptoms of orthorexia nervosa'. *Eating and weight disorders-studies on anorexia, bulimia and obesity*, 1–8.

Page 30: Holland, G. & Tiggemann, M. (2017). 'Strong beats skinny every time: Disordered eating and compulsive exercise in women who post fitspiration on Instagram'. *International Journal of Eating Disorders*, 50(1), 76–79.

Page 33: Boepple, L. & Thompson, J. K. (2014). 'A content analysis of healthy living blogs: Evidence of content thematically consistent with dysfunctional eating attitudes and behaviours'. *International Journal of Eating Disorders*, 47(4), 362–367.

Page 38: Mintel (2014, January 3). 'Dieting in 2014? You're not alone – 24 million Brits have tried to lose weight in the last year'. Mintel. Retrieved from www.mintel.com.

Page 38: Tribole, E. & Resch, E. (2012). 'Principle 1: Reject the dieting mentality'. *Intuitive Eating*. New York: Macmillan, 40–58.

Page 38: de Witt Huberts, J. C., Evers, C. & de Ridder, D. T. (2013). 'Double trouble: Restrained eaters do not eat less and feel worse'. *Psychology & Health*, 28(6), 686–700.

Page 38: Lohse, B., Satter, E., Horacek, T., Gebreselassie, T. & Oakland, M. J. (2007). 'Measuring eating competence: Psychometric properties and validity of the ecSatter Inventory'. *Journal of Nutrition Education and Behavior*, 39(5), S154–S166.

Page 38: López, A. L. O. & Johnson, L. (2016). 'Associations between restrained eating and the size and frequency of overall intake, meal, snack and drink occasions in the UK adult national diet and nutrition survey'. *PloS one*, 11(5), e0156320.

Page 41: Denny, K. N., Loth, K., Eisenberg, M. E. & Neumark-Sztainer, D. (2013). 'Intuitive eating in young adults. Who is doing it, and how is it related to disordered eating behaviours?' *Appetite*, 60, 13–19.

Page 42: Schaefer, J. T. & Magnuson, A. B. (2014). 'A review of interventions that promote eating by internal cues'. *Journal of the Academy of Nutrition and Dietetics*, 114(5), 734–760.

Page 42: Tylka, T. L., Calogero, R. M., & Daníelsdóttir, S. (2015). 'Is intuitive eating the same as flexible dietary control? Their links to each other and well-being could provide an answer'. *Appetite*, 95, 166–175.

Page 42: Gast, J., Nielson, A. C., Hunt, A. & Leiker, J. J. (2015). 'Intuitive eating: associations with physical activity motivation and BMI'. *American Journal of Health Promotion*, 29(3), e91–e99.

Page 45: Kristeller, J., Wolever, R. Q. & Sheets, V. (2014). 'Mindfulness-based eating awareness training (MB-EAT) for binge eating: A randomized clinical trial'. *Mindfulness*, 5(3), 282–297.

Page 47: Chow, C. C. & Hall, K. D. (2014). 'Short and long-term energy intake patterns and their implications for human body weight regulation'. *Physiology & Behavior*, 134, 60–65.

Page 48: Chao, A., Grilo, C. M., White, M. A. & Sinha, R. (2014). 'Food cravings, food intake, and weight status in a community-based sample'. *Eating Behaviors*, 15(3), 478–482.

Page 56: Simpson, C. C. & Mazzeo, S. E. (2017). 'Calorie counting and fitness tracking technology: Associations with eating disorder symptomatology'. *Eating Behaviors*, 26, 89–92.

Page 56: Heymsfield, S. B. & Pietrobelli, A. (2011). 'Individual differences in apparent energy digestibility are larger than generally recognized'. *The American Journal of Clinical Nutrition*, 94(6), 1650–1651.

Page 56: Carmody, R. N. & Wrangham, R. W. (2009). 'The energetic significance of cooking'. *Journal of Human Evolution*, 57(4), 379–391.

Page 56: Tomiyama, A. J., Mann, T., Vinas, D., Hunger, J. M., DeJager, J. & Taylor, S. E. (2010). 'Low calorie dieting increases cortisol'. *Psychosomatic Medicine*, 72(4), 357.

Page 56: Thomas, D. M., Martin, C. K., Lettieri, S. et al. (2013). 'Can a weight loss of one pound a week be achieved with a 3500-kcal deficit? Commentary on a commonly accepted rule'. *International Journal of Obesity*, 37(12), 1611–1613.

Page 56: Sacks, F. M., Bray, G. A., Carey, V. J. et al. (2009). 'Comparison of weight-loss diets with different compositions of fat, protein, and carbohydrates'. *New England Journal of Medicine*, 360(9), 859–873.

Page 56: Dunn, R. (2012, August 27). 'The hidden truth about calories'. *Scientific American*. Retrieved from www.blogs.scientificamerican.com

Page 59: Dietary Guidelines Advisory Committee (2010). 'Report of the dietary guidelines advisory committee on the dietary guidelines for Americans, 2010, to the Secretary of Agriculture and the Secretary of Health and Human Services'. *Agricultural Research Service*.

Page 59: Sacks, F. M., Bray, G. A., Carey, V. J. et al. (2009). 'Comparison of weight-loss diets with different compositions of fat, protein, and carbohydrates'. *New England Journal of Medicine*, 360(9), 859–873.

Page 63: Consumer reports (2014, November). '6 truths about gluten free diet'. Retrieved from www.consumerreports.org.

Page 63: Catassi, C., Gatti, S. & Lionetti, E. (2015). 'World perspective and celiac disease epidemiology'. *Digestive Diseases*, 33(2), 141–146.

Page 65: Drewnowski, A., Mennella, J. A., Johnson, S. L. & Bellisle, F. (2012). 'Sweetness and food preference'. *The Journal of Nutrition*, 142(6), 1142S–1148S.

Page 65: Westwater, M. L., Fletcher, P. C. & Ziauddeen, H. (2016). 'Sugar addiction: The state of the science'. *European Journal of Nutrition*, 55(2), 55–69.

Page 65: Katz, D. L. & Meller, S. (2014). 'Can we say what diet is best for health?' *Annual Review of Public Health*, 35, 83–103.

Page 65: *Vegan Life Magazine* (2016, May). 'Veganism booms by 350%'. Retrieved from www.veganlifemag.com.

Page 65: Graham, J. E., Christian, L. M. & Kiecolt-Glaser, J. K. (2006). 'Stress, age, and immune function: toward a lifespan approach'. *Journal of Behavioural Medicine*, 29(4), 389–400.

Page 68: Pollan, M. (2008). *In Defense of Food: An Eater's Manifesto*. London: Penguin.

Page 68: Key, T. J., Thorogood, M., Appleby, P. N. & Burr, M. L. (1996). 'Dietary habits and mortality in 11000 vegetarians and health-conscious people: Results of a 17 year follow up'. *British Medical Journal*, 313(7060), 775–779.

Page 107: Fritz, C., Ellis, A. M., Demsky, C. A., Lin, B. C. & Guros, F. (2013). 'Embracing work breaks'. *Organizational Dynamics*, 42, 274–280.

Index